Understand the story behind the story this Christmas season with *There Shone a Holy Light*. From the first dawn of creation through the words of the ancient prophets, from the signs and symbols and types to the exact predictions of Jesus' birth, understand afresh the greatest story ever told. This is a book your family will want to have as you celebrate the goodness of this season.

Daniel Darling
Director, Land Center for Cultural Engagement, Southwestern Seminary, Dallas, Texas; Author, *The Characters of Christmas*

It's been said that the Old Testament is like a room full of treasure, but the room is dimly lit. In this daily Advent devotional, Mitch Chase leads us into that great room, finds the dimmer switch, and illuminates the treasure. What better way to prepare for Christmas than to behold, in 25 brilliant reflections, the sparkling glories of the coming Messiah? Let's adore him afresh this year.

Matt Smethurst
Lead pastor, River City Baptist Church, Richmond, Virginia; author, *Tim Keller on the Christian Life*

There Shone a Holy Light

Beholding Christ and Christmas in the Old Testament

Mitchell L. Chase

For my friend Matthew Tellis,
who loves the Christ of Christmas
all year long.

Copyright © Mitchell L. Chase 2025

print ISBN 978-1-5271-1225-4
ebook ISBN 978-1-5271-1333-6

ESV used throughout: Scripture quotations are from The Holy Bible, English Standard Version, copyright © 2001 by Crossway Bibles, a publishing ministry of Good News Publishers. Used by permission. All rights reserved. esv Text Edition: 2011.

10 9 8 7 6 5 4 3 2 1

Published in 2025
by
Christian Focus Publications Ltd,
Geanies House, Fearn, Ross-shire,
IV20 1TW, Great Britain.
www.christianfocus.com

Cover design by Daniel van Straaten

Printed and bound by Gutenberg

All rights reserved. No part of this publication may be reproduced, stored in a retrieval system, or transmitted, in any form, by any means, electronic, mechanical, photocopying, recording or otherwise without the prior permission of the publisher or a licence permitting restricted copying. In the U.K. such licences are issued by the Copyright Licensing Agency, 4 Battlebridge Lane, London, SE1 2HX. www.cla.co.uk

Contents

Acknowledgments 9

Introduction 11

1 The First Adam 13
2 Abel, the Righteous Son 17
3 Noah, the Hope of Lamech 21
4 The Ark That Delivers 25
5 Blessing or Cursing Abraham 29
6 Melchizedek, the Priest-King 33
7 Job, the Blameless Sufferer 37
8 Isaac, the Promised Son and Sacrifice 41
9 The Ladder Uniting Heaven and Earth 45
10 The Humiliation and Exaltation of Joseph 49
11 Moses, the Rejected Prophet and Deliverer 53
12 The Unblemished Lamb 57
13 Israel, the Firstborn Son 61
14 Bread from Heaven 65
15 Water from the Rock 69
16 Immanuel and the Tabernacle 73
17 The Staff of Aaron 77
18 The Bronze Serpent 81
19 The Zeal of Phinehas 85
20 The Saving Name of Joshua 89
21 A Red Cord in the Window 93
22 Samson, the Mighty Judge 97
23 Boaz, the Bethlehem Redeemer 101
24 David, the Singing King.. 105
25 Solomon, the Wise Son of David 109

Contents

Acknowledgments

I love Advent devotionals because I love thinking about the coming of Christ into the world. Can there be news more thrilling than to announce the birth of the Promised One who came to seek and save the lost? Thinking about this news will do much good in us.

When Colin Fast suggested an Advent devotional that explored types of Christ in the Old Testament, I was delighted at the idea. Not only did this project give me an opportunity to reflect at length about the coming of Christ into the world, it also integrated a subject I find deeply edifying to write about and teach—ways in which the Old Testament foreshadows the Messiah. I'm thankful that Colin and the good folks at Christian Focus entrusted me with the project.

My wife Stacie read each devotional to offer feedback, and I'm thankful for the time and energy she spent in these pages. Her support and encouragement make writing a joy. I hope these twenty-five reflections will bless her and my four boys for many years to come.

Acknowledgments

This book is dedicated to Matthew Tellis, my friend for more than a decade, who loves the season of Advent and Christmas like I do. We love the carols and the food, the decorations and the get-togethers. But above all, we delight in the news that the Savior has come, full of grace and truth, to sinners like us. Even when the Christmas season has come to an end, Matthew's love for Christ continues, and rightly so, for Jesus is Lord of all the seasons and weeks of every year.

Introduction

The Bible is a story of light for the darkness because it is the story of Jesus, and he is the light of the world. The opening chapter of Scripture has the famous pronouncement, "'Let there be light,' and there was light" (Gen. 1:3). The closing chapter of Scripture is also about light, but not the kind God creates. John writes about the light that God *is*. He says, "And night will be no more. They will need no light of lamp or sun, for the Lord God will be their light, and they will reign forever and ever" (Rev. 22:5).

Between the light from God at creation and the light of God in the new creation, there is a story of God's good world being plunged into darkness—the darkness of sin and death, of principalities and a raging dragon. And into this darkness God spoke a promise, words about a son who would bring salvation and who would reign in righteousness.

The Old Testament gives signs of this coming redemption. When you read the Old Testament as an unfolding story that anticipates the events in the New, you can see types and shadows of Christ and his redeeming work along the way. There

Introduction

are certainly direct messianic prophecies, like the facts of the Savior being from Israel (Num. 24:17), from the tribe of Judah (Gen. 49:10), from the line of David (2 Sam. 7:12-13), and from the town of Bethlehem (Micah 5:2). But there are also expectations that are more indirect.

Jesus taught that the Old Testament bore witness to him (Luke 24:27, 44-47). And it will be beneficial to our souls when we reflect on the Old Testament people, institutions, and events that foreshadow him. The following twenty-five advent readings are an exploration of Christological types in the Old Testament. As we behold how these ancient stories prepare the way for the Lord, let us read prayerfully and humbly, that our hearts might grow warm in the presence of the everlasting Light (Luke 24:32).

I

The First Adam

The first man was made by God, not born of a mother. This fact of creation is something no other man would ever experience. Even the Lord Jesus was born of a woman.

As the first person whom God made, Adam had a unique role in humanity. He was the head of all people, the first of his kind. Decisions that he made would matter for more than just him.

In the sacred space of Eden, God provided for him, blessing him with a fertile environment to dwell in and to cultivate. Adam was to work it and keep it (Gen. 2:15)—a pair of ideas that occurred later for priests who worked in sacred tabernacle space (Num. 18:5-7). Working it meant service, and keeping it meant guardianship.

Living in Eden involved responsibility and stewardship. Adam would rule, in accordance with the creation mandate in Genesis 1:28. God commissioned His image-bearers to subdue creation and exercise dominion. This call to *subdue* was key to what being an image-bearer meant. Like a king, Adam was to rule. And as an image-bearer, Adam's rule represented the

The First Adam

authority of God. Adam was a king of creation, but this was not a role he seized. It was a role he received.

God gave Adam a prohibition as well. He said, "You may surely eat of every tree of the garden, but of the tree of the knowledge of good and evil you shall not eat, for in the day that you eat of it you shall surely die" (Gen. 2:16-17). This command was for Adam's good, though he didn't uphold it. When Eve gave him a piece of the forbidden fruit, he took it and ate (3:6).

Though Adam and Eve sinned against the Lord, the Lord promised a deliverer, a victor who would defeat the vile and tempting serpent (Gen. 3:15). Faced with temptation, Adam failed in the garden. But the future son of Adam would not fail.

The disobedience of Adam and the obedience of Christ are a vital part of the Apostle Paul's argument in Romans 5. Sin came into the world through one man, and death through sin (Rom. 5:12). But through the righteousness of Christ, sinners can experience justification and eternal life (5:18). Like Adam, Jesus would have a representative role. Jesus was the head of the *new* humanity, the image-bearers who are being restored through their union with the Son of God.

Paul draws a comparison between Adam and Jesus. He says Adam "was a type of the one who was to come" (Rom. 5:14). A correspondence that Adam and Jesus shared was their representative role, also known as their federal headship. In Romans 5:12-21, Paul writes bluntly about Adam's actions. Adam committed transgression (5:14), or sin (5:16). And the result was judgment (5:16), or condemnation (5:16).

The obedience of Christ contrasts with the disobedience of Adam. "For as by the one man's disobedience the many were made sinners, so by the one man's obedience the many will be made righteous" (Rom. 5:19). Though the effects of Adam's

The First Adam

actions were tragic, the effects of Jesus' actions would display the surpassing grace of God toward sinners.

Given the significance of who Jesus is and what he accomplished, Paul called him "the last Adam" (1 Cor. 15:45). In order to understand the depth and breadth of the impact that Jesus' obedience had, we have to see his victory in light of the first Adam's unfaithfulness. The first Adam turned from God's good command, but Jesus upheld and embodied divine wisdom. Jesus was the true and better Adam.

The greatness of Jesus is confirmed by his origin. Paul said, "The first man was from the earth, a man of dust; the second man is from heaven" (1 Cor. 15:47). Paul's claim doesn't deny the incarnation, for Jesus was indeed born of the Virgin Mary. But the incarnation was that of the eternal Son of God, the one by whom and for whom all things were made (Col. 1:16).

Paul's comparisons between the first and last Adams continue. "As was the man of dust, so also are those who are of the dust, and as is the man of heaven, so also are those who are of heaven" (1 Cor. 15:48). What we needed was a new Adam, and the man of heaven is the Adam we needed. If through Adam came sin and condemnation, then through Christ come forgiveness and justification.

The Lord Jesus was born so that he might fulfill the promise of a victorious son who would defeat the serpent (Gen. 3:15). He is the greater Adam whose faithfulness and righteousness would be the refuge for all who come to him by faith. And through faith in Christ, a new and real and everlasting union exists between the sinner and the Savior. Paul said, "Just as we have borne the image of the man of dust, we shall also bear the image of the man of heaven" (1 Cor. 15:49).

The incarnation was for salvation. Christ became like us so that we could become like him. Left to ourselves, we are only

The First Adam

like the first Adam, transgressors who deserve of judgment. Adam was a man of earth, and we are also those of earth. In order to be fitted for heaven and new creation, a greater work was needed that could undo and overcome the scope of the fall. So into the fallen world came the Son of God, full of grace and truth. The Word became flesh because we are flesh.

Mary gave birth to the man of heaven, the last Adam. Just as the phrase "*first* Adam" means there was no representative preceding Adam, so the phrase "*last* Adam" means there will be no Savior beyond Jesus. Paul didn't call Jesus the "next" Adam. He called him the "last Adam."

The advent of Christ was the inauguration of God's kingdom. The promised victory had come, and the man of heaven had been born. The first Adam's transgression would be followed by the last Adam's submission. In the wilderness where Jesus was tempted, he overcame the devil's snares in every case (Matt. 4:1-11).

When that ancient serpent spoke tempting words, they met the holy defiance of the Son of God. Jesus would not waver, and he would not compromise. No doubt the devil remembered how things went with the first Adam in the garden. This time, things would be different. As the incarnate Son of God, the last Adam subdued the evil one and exercised dominion in the wilderness.

2

Abel, the Righteous Son

The first children of our first parents were Cain and Abel. Obeying God's commission in Genesis 1:28, Adam and Eve were fruitful and multiplied. The birth of sons was especially significant in light of the promise in Genesis 3:15, where Adam and Eve learned that a son would be born who would crush the serpent. And now they had two sons. Could one of these be the promised victor?

Time passed as these boys grew. An occasion came for presenting offerings, and Cain brought fruit from the ground, while Abel brought the firstborn of his flock (Gen. 4:3-4). The kind of offerings corresponded to the nature of Cain and Abel's work, for Cain worked the ground and Abel was a keeper of sheep (4:2).

Though both brothers presented offerings, they were not received in the same way. The Lord looks beneath the sacrifice and beholds the worshiper. The heart is not hidden by the

Abel, the Righteous Son

offering. We learn that "the Lord had regard for Abel and his offering, but for Cain and his offering he had no regard" (Gen. 4:4-5). The offering represents the worshiper. If God rejects the offering, he is rejecting the worshiper.

Perhaps the problem was the kind of sacrifice that Cain brought. Should he have brought an offering from the flock, like his brother Abel did? While the problem could have been the kind of offering, the text does not make this clear. It is possible that the Lord did not regard Cain's offering because of Cain's heart. After all, the Israelites were permitted to bring offerings from the ground as well as from the flock (Lev. 1-7). In the pre-Israelite days of Cain and Abel, apparently both ground and flock offerings were brought to the Lord.

Rather than focusing on the kind of offering, we should focus on the kind of worshiper. When God did not regard Cain and the offering he'd brought, Cain did not display confusion or penitence or devotion. He was "very angry, and his face fell" (Gen. 4:5). Cain was unrighteous, and sin was crouching like a predator seeking to devour him (4:7). He spoke to his brother Abel (4:8), though we don't know what he said. The result of the conversation was the two of them together in a field. Suddenly, Cain rose up against Abel and killed him (4:8).

Abel had done nothing wrong, according to the text. The evildoer was Cain. The first death recorded in Scripture was a murder, and it was the murder of Adam's son. This turn of events is especially devastating when we remember the promise of a victorious son of Eve who would crush the serpent (Gen. 3:15). Of the two sons, Cain and Abel, neither would be the serpent crusher. In fact, the righteous son was overcome by the wicked one! With Genesis 3:15 casting a shadow over Genesis 4, the serpentine actions of Cain resulted in the defeat of Abel, the seed of the woman.

Abel, the Righteous Son

Abel is the first righteous sufferer in the biblical storyline. Though Abel was not sinless, his death was still not a reaping of what he had sown. Abel worshiped the Lord; he offered sacrifices to the Lord, and he died at the hands of his unrighteous sibling. The hostility of Cain toward Abel was a manifestation of the spiritual conflict between the seed of the serpent and the seed of the woman.

The Lord said to Cain, "Where is Abel your brother?" (Gen. 4:9). And Cain's response was flippant, dismissive: "I do not know; am I my brother's keeper?" (4:9). The Lord's question drew out Cain's hardhearted answer. This brother's words revealed his spiritual rebellion, just as the premeditated murder revealed his unrighteous hatred. Abel's blood cried out from the ground for justice (Gen. 4:10). Wickedness needed a reckoning, and the God of justice heard the cry for it.

The suffering of righteous Abel is the beginning of a pattern of righteous sufferers, a pattern that includes people like Job, Joseph, and Daniel. And this pattern reached its greatest significance in the life of the Lord Jesus. Morally blameless and altogether righteous, Jesus faced the rejection of his brothers and his Israelite kinsmen. He came to his own, and his own received him not (John 1:11; 7:5).

When Jesus died, he fulfilled the enmity prophesied in Genesis 3:15. The serpent struck his heel, but he crushed its head. The death of Abel cried out for divine justice, while the death of Jesus satisfied divine justice. Jesus is the mediator of a new covenant, and his blood "speaks a better word than the blood of Abel" (Heb. 12:24). The voice of this better word is the plea for mercy toward sinners because justice has been satisfied through the substitutionary sacrifice of the righteous Son of God. Abel offered a sacrifice from his flock, while Jesus offered himself. Jesus was the greater Abel offering a greater sacrifice.

Abel, the Righteous Son

The promised seed of the woman would be the suffering Son of Man. Jesus taught his disciples, "The Son of Man is going to be delivered into the hands of men, and they will kill him. And when he is killed, after three days he will rise" (Mark 9:31). His death would result from the manifest hatred of the seed of the serpent who wanted his destruction.

Jesus is the righteous sufferer whose death heralds salvation. And through faith in him, we belong to him. He is unashamed to call us his brothers (Heb. 2:11). We receive his shepherding care, his steadfast love, and his everlasting life. He was born that he might bring us to himself, bringing many sons to glory (Heb. 2:10). He came to be his brother's keeper.

3

Noah, the Hope of Lamech

When you think of Noah, you surely think of the ark-builder and flood-survivor, but his father Lamech had a different hope for him. Before God made a promise of a worldwide deluge, Lamech was going to have a son, and he thought carefully about the name.

Genesis 5:28-29 says, "When Lamech had lived 182 years, he fathered a son and called his name Noah, saying, 'Out of the ground that the Lord has cursed, this one shall bring us relief from our work and from the painful toil of our hands.'"

Lamech's hope for Noah was that he would be the promised son foretold in Genesis 3:15. In Genesis 3:15, God told the serpent, "I will put enmity between you and the woman, and between your offspring and her offspring; he shall bruise your head, and you shall bruise his heel." The future son would defeat the serpent.

Noah, the Hope of Lamech

The son's victory would also have an effect on the cursed state of the world. The Lord had told Adam, "Cursed is the ground because of you; in pain you shall eat of it all the days of your life; thorns and thistles it shall bring forth for you; and you shall eat the plants of the field. By the sweat of your face you shall eat bread, till you return to the ground, for out of it you were taken; for you are dust, and to dust you shall return" (Gen. 3:17-19).

The cursed ground could not be overcome by all the toil of man. Man's toil would end with death in the dust. But Lamech's hope was that a son would be born whose work would overcome the curse. Lamech said that "this one shall bring us relief from our work and from the painful toil of our hands" (Gen. 5:29). The future serpent-crusher would be a curse-reverser. He would bring "relief" to those who faced the toil and pain of living in a fallen world.

Noah's name is like the Hebrew word for "rest," so Lamech has connected his son's name to the hope of sinners, the hope that a future son would bring rest to the world. The curse upon the ground and the toilsome nature of work are indicators of a groaning and restless world. Paul wrote that "the whole creation has been groaning together in the pains of childbirth until now" (Rom. 8:22). The groaning is for rest, and this rest would look like redemption.

As the story in Genesis 6–8 unfolds, the reader learns that Noah is not the son foretold in Genesis 3:15. However, as a righteous man whose obedience leads to the deliverance of others, Noah is a type of Christ. He foreshadows the One whose perfect life and work would bring rest and redemption. Lamech's hope, then, was not in vain. His son was a sign pointing forward to a redeemer.

In Genesis 6, we learn that "Noah was a righteous man, blameless in his generation. Noah walked with God" (Gen. 6:9).

Noah, the Hope of Lamech

God gave instructions to Noah about building the ark, and Noah "did all that God commanded him" (6:22). Noah's righteousness was demonstrated in obedience, and he stood out among his wicked and crooked generation. Whereas "the wickedness of man was great in the earth" and "every intention of the thoughts of his heart was only evil continually" (6:5), the biblical author tells us that Noah communed with the Lord (6:9).

Peter told his readers that Noah was "a herald of righteousness" (2 Pet. 2:5). Calling Noah a "herald" draws attention to words, because heralds—or preachers—*proclaim* something. Noah was no silent ark-builder. He lived in a generation that needed to know of God's righteousness and wrath. Noah was a herald for the Lord and of the Lord, but his message fell upon deaf ears.

Lamech, along with others who worshiped the Lord, hoped for the future son who would defeat the serpent and reverse the curse. But his son Noah did not fulfill this redemptive role. After the judgment of the flood, the serpent remained uncrushed, and the curse remained in place. Those who left the ark re-emerged into a fallen world. Though the ark "came to rest on the mountains of Ararat" (Gen. 8:4), this rest didn't relieve God's image-bearers from toil.

The Lord Jesus was born to fulfill the hope of Lamech. According to Luke 3, Jesus was a descendant of "Noah, the son of Lamech" (Luke 3:36). Jesus was a herald of the kingdom; he communed with the Father, and he lived a righteous life in a crooked and wayward generation. Through his obedience and sacrifice, he offers rest for the weary, redemption for sinners. We cannot toil enough to deliver ourselves from the judgment due upon our sins, but we can rejoice in the One who liberates us from the curse.

Jesus liberates us from the curse upon the ground by bearing the curse of sin upon the cross. The thorns of Genesis 3:18

Noah, the Hope of Lamech

were bent into a crown, and this crown of thorns was pressed onto his head. And now we, in Christ, become heralds of righteousness—heralds of *his* righteousness. We proclaim to a perishing world that Jesus died and was raised imperishable, and the accomplishment of his atoning work is counted to any who come to him by faith.

Looking to Christ, we await his return, which shall be sudden like the watery judgment in the days of Noah. Jesus said, "For as were the days of Noah, so will be the coming of the Son of Man. For as in those days before the flood they were eating and drinking, marrying and giving in marriage, until the day when Noah entered the ark, and they were unaware until the flood came and swept them all away, so will be the coming of the Son of Man" (Matt. 24:37-39).

The Lord Jesus who came will come again, and his second advent will complete what he began. All will be well, for he will flood the earth with his blessing and overcome the effects of the curse upon God's good world. The Son of Man is the greater Noah who will answer the groans of creation with his power of redemption. Only One who reigns supreme is worthy of our trust and devotion. The name "Noah" points to the Name that is above every name.

4

The Ark That Delivers

There was only one hope to be saved from the judgment of the flood, and that was to be inside the ark. If you were inside the ark, you were delivered. If you were outside the ark, you perished.

The ark itself was to be a massive three-story boat that could hold a male and female creature of every kind (Gen. 6:19-20). In addition to these animals, Noah, his wife, his three sons, and his sons' wives would be aboard (6:18).

When Noah was six hundred years old, the eight people entered the ark "to escape the waters of the flood" (Gen. 7:7). "And the Lord shut him in" (7:16). Sealed and protected by the Lord, the ark rose as the waters increased, and it floated on the surface of the waters (7:17-18). The waters receded, and the ark came to rest on the mountains of Ararat (8:4). After spending a year on the ark, the people and animals disembarked (8:18-19).

The presence of the ark bobbing in and out of the water during the watery downpour and uprising was a bright light

The Ark That Delivers

of hope in a dark time of judgment. Because of the extensive number of people alive at the time of the flood, probably not everyone would have seen the ark when the rain came. But many would have seen it. Many would have been caught up in the dreadful judgment and realized that those within that boat were in the only safe place on earth.

Consider the visibility of Noah's whole venture. The ark was no small boat. It was approximately 450 feet long, 75 feet wide, and 45 feet high. Such a vessel would have taken months to build, and there was no way such a project could be kept private. The materials that were needed, and the time required for construction, would mean a persevering ark-builder and some perplexed onlookers and naysayers. Now imagine the train of animals. This line of creatures, preparing to board the ark, would be an unconcealable sight.

How much scorn did others heap upon Noah as they saw what he was doing? How much revilement and headshaking from others did he endure? How much confusion and disbelief went through the minds of those who heard the swinging hammer and who watched the crawling and walking and flying creatures?

Yet Noah built. The Lord had promised that a watery judgment would come, and being the kind of man who walked with the Lord, Noah believed his words. The writer of Hebrews said, "By faith Noah, being warned by God concerning events as yet unseen, in reverent fear constructed an ark for the saving of his household" (Heb. 11:7). As people saw the massive ark being built, they were watching the only refuge that would deliver anyone from the flood.

The reason Noah's ark points us to Christ is because Christ is the only refuge from the judgment of God. The floodwaters of wrath threaten to overwhelm and consume us. Where can safety be found? We need to be sealed in the ark which is Christ

The Ark That Delivers

Jesus. We need to be "shut in" by the Holy Spirit. United with Christ, we will not be crushed by future condemnation. Jesus is our place of refuge, our ark.

Throughout the book of Psalms, the Lord is the refuge and fortress for his people. He is their place of deliverance, their high tower and rock (see, for example, Ps. 31:1-5). Only fitting, then, is the truth that God gave his Son to be the refuge—the ark—for sinners.

God has warned us of coming wrath upon the wicked, and he has provided the refuge of his Son. In Psalm 2 we read, "Kiss the Son, lest he be angry, and you perish in the way, for his wrath is quickly kindled. Blessed are all who take refuge in him" (Ps. 2:12). If Noah and his family were blessed to be inside the ark, then how much more is the person blessed who flees to Christ as the Savior of sinners.

The fury and purity of divine justice will not fall upon the people of God. We have been sealed in Christ, and this seal cannot be broken. The New Covenant shall withstand the outpouring of judgment at the end of all things. Our spiritual ark shall not leak or collapse. We are secure in the Son.

In Genesis 6–8, eight people "were brought safely through water. Baptism, which corresponds to this, now saves you, not as a removal of dirt from the body but as an appeal to God for a good conscience, through the resurrection of Jesus Christ, who has gone into heaven and is at the right hand of God, with angels, authorities, and powers having been subjected to him" (1 Pet. 3:20-22).

Noah's family needed to be safely brought through the waters of judgment, and that is our need as well—to be brought safely through the end-time judgment of God. Our baptism is our public appeal, our submission to the Christ who subjects all things to himself. Baptism is the declaration that because of the

The Ark That Delivers

death and resurrection of Christ, we have been brought safely through the waters of judgment.

The waters of judgment will not consume us, because they consumed Jesus for us. Jesus suffered on the cross "once for sins, the righteous for the unrighteous, that he might bring us to God" (1 Pet. 3:18). Having satisfied the judgment of God as our faithful substitute, Jesus can be the faithful refuge for all who come to him for deliverance.

The one whom Mary carried was born to carry us through the waters of judgment. And he carries us still. United to the Son and sealed by the Spirit, we will come to rest with Christ on the mountains of the new creation, where the glory of the Son will forever shine and judgment shall be no more.

5

Blessing or Cursing Abraham

There was once an old man who left everything he'd ever known in order to follow the Lord who came to him first. As the martyr Stephen put it, "The God of glory appeared to our father Abraham when he was in Mesopotamia, before he lived in Haran, and said to him, 'Go out from your land and from your kindred and go into the land that I will show you'" (Acts 7:2-3).

Abraham journeyed to the land of Canaan, which would later become the land of Israel because of God's promise. God would bless Abraham and make him a blessing: "And I will make of you a great nation, and I will bless you and make your name great, so that you will be a blessing. I will bless those who bless you, and him who dishonors you I will curse, and in you all the families of the earth shall be blessed" (Gen. 12:2-3).

The worldwide scope of blessing is important because of the worldwide scope of the curse. In Genesis 3, the Lord says to the serpent, "Cursed are you..." (Gen. 3:14). He says to Adam,

Blessing or Cursing Abraham

"Cursed is the ground because of you..." (3:17). He says to Cain, "And now you are cursed from the ground..." (4:11). Lamech said the ground was "cursed" (5:29), and Noah said, "Cursed be Canaan..." (9:25).

The five uses of the word "curse" in Genesis 1–11 are followed by five occurrences of the word "bless" (or blessing/blessed) in Genesis 12:2-3. God has promised to bless the world that suffers under the curse. This promise of blessing is good news for a broken world and a corrupt people. Only the blessing of God can overcome the problem of sin and death.

How does Abraham fit into all of this? God tells him, "In you all the families of the earth shall be blessed" (Gen. 12:3). The line of Abraham will be messianic because the distant son of Abraham is the Lord Jesus. The families of the earth will be blessed in Abraham because the Messiah will be born from Abraham.

God's promise of blessing is not the only thing the patriarch learns about. There is judgment promised as well. God tells him, "I will bless those who bless you, and him who dishonors you I will curse" (Gen. 12:3). People will be blessed or cursed, depending on how they respond to Abraham. They will reap what they sow. If they bless Abraham, they will be blessed. But if they dishonor Abraham, they will be cursed.

In the stories that follow Genesis 12, we learn that dishonoring Abraham involves opposing him and rejecting him—or opposing and rejecting the seed of Abraham. Such dishonor is folly because it brings the curse of God. The enemies of Abraham are enemies of God, and the enemies of God get crushed.

According to Genesis 12, then, how you relate to Abraham signals your spiritual posture toward the Lord. Does this make you think of what Jesus taught about himself? Near the end of the Sermon on the Mount (Matt. 5–7), Jesus spoke of future judgment and future vindication. And what happens in the

Blessing or Cursing Abraham

future depends on what people do with the words of Jesus now. He is the great dividing line, the one whose teachings reveal who is the fool and who is the wise.

Jesus said, "Everyone then who hears these words of mine and does them will be like a wise man who built his house on the rock. And the rain fell, and the floods came, and the winds blew and beat on that house, but it did not fall, because it had been founded on the rock. And everyone who hears these words of mine and does not do them will be like a foolish man who built his house on the sand. And the rain fell, and the floods came, and the winds blew and beat against that house, and it fell, and great was the fall of it" (Matt. 7:24-27).

Hearing and doing, or hearing and not doing: these are the two options, and the results are either blessing or cursing. The ultimate blessing is our lives being vindicated at the final judgment, when the rain and floods and winds come. The words of Jesus are like a solid rock for building your life, and only that sure foundation will endure the wrath of God, for Jesus himself satisfied divine justice on the cross in our place. The ultimate curse, though, is when the rain and floods and winds blow upon the life that was built on a foundation other than the Lord Jesus. All other ground is sinking sand, and the final judgment will make that clear.

People were to honor Abraham, but only Jesus is worthy of all blessing and honor and glory and power. People were to bless Abraham, but only Jesus is worthy of worldwide worship and adoration. God promised Abraham that through him he would bless the world. Jesus is greater than Abraham because Jesus *is* the blessing that came into the world. He is the blessing that came to reverse the curse.

God told Abraham, "I will bless you and make your name great" (Gen. 12:2), and that promise is most truly fulfilled in

Blessing or Cursing Abraham

Christ. He is the blessed Son of Abraham, and he is the blessing for the families of the earth. He is the one with a great name—a name greater than Abraham's. Jesus has the name above every name, that at his name everyone should bow.

For those ready to trust the Son, the blessing of life is theirs already. Because the life of believers is founded on the rock which is Jesus' words, they are even now secure in him. Christ was born into a world that was under the curse of sin and death. And he came to bring blessing to reverse the curse, pardon to cancel sin, and life to overthrow death.

6

Melchizedek, the Priest-King

Abraham met a mysterious man in the land of Canaan, a man whose name appears only twice in the whole Old Testament—once in Genesis 14 and once in Psalm 110. Yet the scarcity of mentions does not signal unimportance. According to the writer of Hebrews, the man known as Melchizedek was very important indeed.

After Abraham rescued Lot from some ancient Near Eastern kings, there was a noteworthy encounter in a place called Salem (later known as Jeru*salem*). The encounter seemed unexpected after a report of warfare, and no biblical narrative beforehand or afterward told of Abraham's encounter with such a man. Suddenly, into the scene we read that "Melchizedek king of Salem brought out bread and wine. (He was priest of God Most High.) And he blessed him and said, 'Blessed be Abram by God Most High, Possessor of heaven and earth; and blessed be God

Melchizedek, the Priest-King

Most High, who has delivered your enemies into your hand!' And Abram gave him a tenth of everything" (Gen. 14:18-20).

The name Melchizedek means "king of righteousness." But he was not only a king. The biblical author says the man was "priest of God Most High," which means he was a true priest. There were pagan priests in the ancient world, but Melchizedek was a priest of God. This mediating role was prior to the Levitical priesthood and prior to the tabernacle. In the city of Salem, Melchizedek was a priestly king, a royal mediator.

Melchizedek approached Abraham with food and drink, "bread and wine" (Gen. 14:18). This action and those items were a show of hospitality and fellowship. And the king-priest blessed the patriarch. After Abraham tithed to Melchizedek, the scene between them ended.

The next and last place in the Old Testament where Melchizedek's name appears is Psalm 110, a psalm of David. Writing about the future Messiah, David reports the words of God to the coming king: "Sit at my right hand, until I make your enemies your footstool" (Ps. 110:1). Not only will this figure be a king, he will also be a priest. David writes, again, words from God to the coming king: "You are a priest forever after the order of Melchizedek" (Ps. 110:4). In a single psalm, David has written about the future Messiah as both king and priest, and that combination of roles is like Melchizedek in Genesis 14, for he was a king-priest in Salem.

Moving to the New Testament, only one book mentions Melchizedek. The author of Hebrews incorporates this Old Testament figure into a key argument in the letter. Jesus is the promised king from the Old Testament, and he is also a priest whose perfect sacrifice and mediation are central to the good news of the gospel. But, as the writer of Hebrews notes, Jesus is not from Israel's priestly tribe, which was Levi (Heb. 7:13-14).

Melchizedek, the Priest-King

Jesus is from the tribe of Judah, "and in connection with that tribe Moses said nothing about priests" (7:14).

Jesus' priesthood is not a Levitical one. He is both king and priest, and that reality reminds us not of Aaron (and Aaron's descendants) but of Melchizedek. The writer is clear on this point: Jesus is a priest who "arises in the likeness of Melchizedek" (Heb. 7:15). Following the writer's argument, we can see that, while Melchizedek in Genesis isn't Christ, he is a type of Christ.

The Lord Jesus came into the world to be the king and priest whom we need. Old Testament priests occupied their priestly office on the basis of their bodily descent (Heb. 7:16), but genealogy was not a factor for the priestly role of Christ. The irrelevance of a priestly genealogy was like Melchizedek's situation in Genesis 14, for the biblical author introduced him without referring to the man's father or mother. Because of this omission, it's as if Melchizedek "is without father or mother or genealogy, having neither beginning of days nor end of life" (Heb. 7:3). The writer isn't saying Melchizedek was never born or never died. He's simply noting what isn't reported in the story involving Melchizedek.

The author of Hebrews notes other elements in the Genesis 14 account. He says that Abraham tithed to the king-priest (Heb. 7:4) and received the king-priest's blessing (7:7). The actions of tithing and blessing identify Abraham as the inferior and Melchizedek as the superior, for Melchizedek pronounced the blessing and Abraham offered the tithe. Abraham's action was an acknowledgment of Melchizedek's superiority, and the writer of Hebrews argues for a long-term significance in that action. Since Levitical priests descended, eventually, from Abraham, and since Abraham acknowledged Melchizedek's superiority, "One might even say that Levi himself, who receives tithes,

Melchizedek, the Priest-King

paid tithes through Abraham, for he was still in the loins of his ancestor when Melchizedek met him" (Heb. 7:9-10).

Jesus' priesthood is not only different from the Levitical priests; it is *better*. If the earlier priests were mediators in the Sinai Covenant, Jesus' priesthood is part of a new and better covenant (Heb. 7:22). He "continues forever" (7:24) because of his resurrection of the dead. When the Levitical priests died, their inferior priesthood came to an end.

Jesus referred to his "new covenant" work when he ate the last supper with his disciples. In Luke 22, he took the bread and the cup and spoke of his body and blood being given for his disciples (22:19-20). The first time bread and wine were associated with a meal was in Genesis 14, where Melchizedek "brought out bread and wine" for fellowship with Abraham. Many centuries later, Jesus sat at a table with bread and wine and spoke of the new covenant he was going to establish. He was the priest-king who fulfilled the pattern of Salem's ancient king. Jesus would have an everlasting priesthood. He was born to bring people to God. Paul said, "For there is one God, and there is one mediator between God and men, the man Christ Jesus" (1 Tim. 2:5). Jesus was the true and greater "king of righteousness" (Heb. 7:2), a "priest forever after the order of Melchizedek" (Ps. 110:4).

7

Job, the Blameless Sufferer

In the land of Uz, there was a man called Job, who had everything ... and then lost everything. His story is agonizing because the initial blessings were so great and the loss was so severe. According to the narrator of the story, Job was a blameless man, upright, someone who feared the Lord (Job 1:1). And in the eyes of the people of the east, Job was blessed. He had a big family; he possessed many livestock, and he exercised spiritual oversight and attentiveness as the patriarch (1:2-5).

But the devil believed that Job's reverence for God was due to the blessed circumstances of Job's family and possessions. Satan told the Lord, "Stretch out your hand and touch all that he has, and he will curse you to your face" (Job 1:11). This God-fearing man then experienced the systematic losses of his servants, his livestock, and his children (1:13-19). Job cried out, "Naked I came from my mother's womb, and naked shall I return. The

Job, the Blameless Sufferer

Lord gave, and the Lord has taken away; blessed be the name of the Lord" (1:21).

Though Job had faced unimaginable tragedy, he then endured physical affliction (Job 2:7-8) and the foolishness of his wife's exhortation to curse God and die (2:9). Yet Job acknowledged the mysterious sovereignty of God and did not turn from him (1:21-22; 2:10). Job's friends arrived to comfort him with their presence, and they stayed silent for a week (2:12–13). But apparently, these friends felt frustration building inside them, as they prepared to channel words of accusation against their friend, and the pressure began to release in a series of speeches.

Because of how the book of Job opened, we know that the man's suffering was not due to any rebellion against the Lord. On the contrary, he feared the Lord and turned from evil (Job 1:1). Like Abel, Job was a righteous sufferer. Yet Job's friends operated with an exclusive theology of retribution: those who suffer are reaping consequences for wickedness. But, while sinning against the Lord can certainly bring consequences (such as affliction), the presence of affliction in a person's life is no guarantee of some deep-seated spiritual rebellion. Eliphaz, Bildad, and Zophar are too confident in their claims, and their comfort is compromised by their accusations. In their assessment of Job's suffering, they didn't seem to have a category for "the suffering of the righteous."

Job's affliction ends with vindication. In the last chapter of the story, God's anger burns against the three friends (Job 42:7) because they did not speak what was right (42:8). Job offered prayers on behalf of his friends, and the Lord accepted this intercession (42:9). And after Job had prayed for those who had falsely accused him, the Lord restored his fortunes and gave him twice as much as he had at the start

Job, the Blameless Sufferer

of the story (42:10). So "the latter days of Job" were blessed "more than his beginning" (42:12).

Jesus of Nazareth was born to fulfill the pattern (or type) of the righteous sufferer. He is a true and greater Job. While the people of the east viewed Job as greatly blessed, none was more blessed than the eternal Son. And none experienced greater suffering, as the Lord Jesus satisfied divine justice in our place. He was truly blameless and took our blame.

According to the four Gospels, Jesus faced false accusers. People accused him of blasphemy (Mark 2:7) and of doing miracles by the power of the devil (3:22). On the night Jesus stood before the Jewish authorities, false witnesses rose up against him (14:56-57). Jesus knew what it was like to be accused by those who should have trusted him and supported him. One of the twelve even betrayed him! Judas Iscariot made a deal with the Jewish leaders to betray Jesus for money (14:10-11).

Just as Job's accusers were shown to be false, Jesus' accusers ultimately failed as well. Their opposition was in vain, for he rose from the dead on the third day. His affliction was great, but it led to vindication. The vindicated Son rose in a glorified body—a state that was greater than his mortal body at birth. His bodily resurrection meant embodied immortality. Job's final days were greater than when the story began (Job 42:10), and the same is true for Jesus. The Jewish leadership and Roman soldiers killed the author of life, but God raised him from the dead (Acts 3:14-15).

While Job's character was upright (Job 1:1), he was still a sinner. Jesus was *without* sin (Heb. 4:15). His thoughts, desires, words, and actions were never faulty. Furthermore, Jesus was a great mediator, an effective intercessor. Job's prayers were effective on behalf of his friends (Job 42:8-9), but only Jesus was and is the perfect advocate. John gives us some assurance in this

Job, the Blameless Sufferer

regard: "If anyone does sin, we have an advocate with the Father, Jesus Christ the righteous" (1 John 2:1). Jesus is able to "save to the uttermost those who draw near to God through him, since he always lives to make intercession for them" (Heb. 7:25).

But all of Jesus' effective intercession is rooted in who he *is*. The angel told Mary, "You will conceive in your womb and bear a son, and you shall call his name Jesus" (Luke 1:31). And "the child to be born will be called holy—the Son of God" (1:35). The Lord Jesus was born so that we would be holy in him, that we would be vindicated in him, that we would be children of God in union with him.

The righteous indignation of God does not rest on us, because on the cross the blameless and righteous sufferer bore this wrath. Though Job died "an old man" and "full of days" (Job 42:17), Jesus rose an immortal man and full of unending days. The greatness of Jesus is now evident in his effectual prayers, his priestly intercession, his unceasing advocacy for his people. He reigns as the eternal friend and mediator of the saints.

8

Isaac, the Promised Son and Sacrifice

In Genesis 3:15, Eve learned that she would have a descendant who would defeat the serpent. The words were from God, so they were a divine promise. And because this promise was from God, the son from Eve would surely come. One of the ways this promise was sustained throughout the Old Testament is through the birth of important figures. In fact, whenever a biblical author reports a prophesied birth, readers should lean in and pay attention.

Abraham received a promise of a son. Though he was an old man, he learned that God would give him and his wife Sarah a son (Gen. 17:15-16). At first, the notion seemed ludicrous. Abraham laughed and asked, "Shall a child be born to a man who is a hundred years old? Shall Sarah, who is ninety years old, bear a child?" (17:17). Yet God's design was to defy human expectations. Though Sarah was barren, and though she and Abraham were old, God was going to do what man could not do.

Isaac, the Promised Son and Sacrifice

In addition to promising a son, the Lord told Abraham what the name would be. God said, "You shall call his name Isaac. I will establish my covenant with him as an everlasting covenant for his offspring after him" (Gen. 17:19). The conception of this son would demonstrate the power of God, for Abraham and Sarah had been unable to have any children together (11:30). At the appointed time, Sarah conceived and bore a son (21:2). Abraham was 100 years old and Sarah was 90, but they had a newborn. And as God had said, they named the boy Isaac.

God had the power to fulfill the promises he made. He was not dependent on the abilities of his image bearers. He could *enable* them, which is what he did in Abraham and Sarah's case. If God made the heavens and the earth, he was certainly able to overcome the barrenness of Sarah's womb.

Isaac was to bear the covenant promises (Gen. 17:19), just as his father Abraham did. Imagine the patriarch's surprise, then, when God gave an instruction that involved the boy's death. While Isaac was still young, the Lord told Abraham, "Take your son, your only son Isaac, whom you love, and go to the land of Moriah, and offer him there as a burnt offering on one of the mountains of which I shall tell you" (Gen. 22:2). At this point, Isaac had no children. The death of Isaac would seem, therefore, to bring an end to the covenant line.

Nevertheless, Abraham took Isaac to the land of Moriah (Gen. 22:3). Arriving at the spot, Abraham told the men who had traveled with him, "Stay here with the donkey; I and the boy will go over there and worship and come again to you" (22:5). This was no ruse. Abraham intended to go up that mountain with Isaac and to come back with him as well. He already knew of God's power to enable a barren womb to conceive, and he trusted that God could raise the dead boy whom he had asked Abraham to sacrifice (see Heb. 11:19). He

Isaac, the Promised Son and Sacrifice

knew that God would keep his promises, and those promises included the designation of Isaac as the covenant-bearer who would have offspring of his own (Gen. 21:12).

Abraham and Isaac walked up the mountain. And when the time of sacrifice had come, the angel of Yahweh commanded Abraham to stop (Gen. 22:11-12). A ram, which was caught in the brush nearby, would be the sacrifice instead of Abraham's son. The laying down and taking up of Isaac's body was a figurative resurrection from the dead (Heb. 11:19).

Though Isaac did not die as a sacrifice that day, the day would come when another promised Son would lay down his life. Jesus is the greater son of Abraham (Matt. 1:1), a new Isaac. Jesus' birth and name were prophesied, and the angelic message came to a young virgin in Nazareth, named Mary. The angel said, "You will conceive in your womb and bear a son, and you shall call his name Jesus" (Luke 1:31).

But, compared with barren women in the Old Testament who conceived, something was extraordinarily different in Mary's situation. She was unmarried and a virgin. She even asked the angel how God would bring to pass this promise (Luke 1:34). The child in Mary's womb would be the work of the Holy Spirit (1:35). And the angel reminded her, "Nothing will be impossible with God" (1:37).

Unlike Isaac's birth, Jesus' birth was the fulfillment of the promise in Genesis 3:15. Isaac's birth foreshadowed it, however. At the appointed time, the Lord Jesus was born, and he was both the promised Son and the perfect sacrifice. Isaac had been spared by the ram caught in thorns, but no such provision was made for Christ. He would be the Father's Son, who would lay down his life in order to take it up again (John 10:18).

The apostle Paul identified Jesus as the seed of Abraham, in whom we have inheritance. He told the Galatians, "Now the

Isaac, the Promised Son and Sacrifice

promises were made to Abraham and to his offspring. It does not say, 'And to offsprings,' referring to many, but referring to one, 'And to your offspring,' who is Christ" (Gal. 3:16). Interpreting the Old Testament, Paul rightly sees that Christ—not Isaac—is the fulfillment of God's promise to Abraham.

Christ Jesus is the son through whom the families of the earth will be blessed. He is the heir in whom we are also heirs. He is the seed, the son, who will possess the gate of his enemies (Gen. 22:17-18). As Jesus was a son of promise, we are—by faith—children of promise too (Gal. 4:28). We are children of promise because our standing with God is not the result of the flesh. Rather, the Spirit has accomplished a work of regeneration and salvation in us. The same Spirit who overshadowed the womb of Mary has brought life to our hearts. And now, through faith in the promised Son, we are promised sons and daughters.

9

The Ladder Uniting Heaven and Earth

Abraham had Isaac, Isaac had Jacob, and Jacob had ... a dream. When he had this particular dream, his life had already taken some challenging turns, and these troubles were of his own making. He had deceived his father and brother and stolen his brother Esau's birthright and blessing (Gen. 25 and 27). He even had to leave the land of Israel because Esau wanted to kill him (Gen. 27:41-45).

In Genesis 28, Jacob left Beersheba to travel; one night, he lay down on a stone to sleep (Gen. 28:10-11). And there, Jacob dreamed: "behold, there was a ladder set up on the earth, and the top of it reached to heaven. And behold, the angels of God were ascending and descending on it!" (28:12).

The Ladder Uniting Heaven and Earth

For the reader of Genesis, this description of the ladder is reminiscent of the Tower of Babel (Gen. 11:1-9). In that earlier story, inhabitants in the ancient Near East had said, "Come, let us build ourselves a city and a tower with its top in the heavens, and let us make a name for ourselves, lest we be dispersed over the face of the whole earth" (11:4). In the tower story and in Jacob's dream, there is something reaching toward heaven. The Babel tower, however, was the construction of man. The ladder was something else. In 28:12, the ladder was "set up on the earth," and the implication is that it was set up *by God*. Here, at last, is a connection between heaven and earth. While God's disapproval was evident in the Babel story (11:5-9), no such disapproval is found in Jacob's dream of the ladder.

Ancient worshipers understood heaven and earth to be separate, so connecting them seemed to be a desirable task. If achieved, such connection would mean contact with the divine, communion with what is beyond this world. Jacob's dream was about the uniting of heaven and earth.

The ladder in Genesis 28 was occupied: "the angels of God were ascending and descending on it!" (28:12). The presence of angels confirms the uniting of heaven and earth, for these heavenly beings were traversing the ladder. Remarkably, in 28:13 we read that the Lord "stood above it." Jacob's dream was of a theophany, a divine manifestation. The translation in 28:13 could even be that the Lord "stood beside him," referring to Jacob. Such a rendering would mean that the ladder marked the descent of the divine to earth, resulting in a close encounter with Jacob. Or 28:13 could mean that the Lord "stood upon it," visualizing the Lord upon the ladder—an image that still denotes descent for an encounter with Jacob.

The Lord's voice promised that Jacob would have offspring and would inherit the land of Canaan (Gen. 28:13-14). These

The Ladder Uniting Heaven and Earth

promises echo what God had promised first to Abraham and then to Isaac. Jacob, too, would bear the covenant promises. Even though Jacob was leaving the Promised Land for a time, God said, "Behold, I am with you and will keep you wherever you go, and will bring you back to this land. For I will not leave you until I have done what I have promised you" (28:15). Therefore, Jacob's flight from Canaan was not the end of his story with that land.

When Jacob awoke, he said, "Surely the Lord is in this place, and I did not know it" (Gen. 28:16). He named the place Bethel, which means "house of God" (28:19). He said, "How awesome is this place! This is none other than the house of God, and this is the gate of heaven" (28:17). Not only had Jacob encountered the Lord and received divine promises and assurances, he had dreamed of this ladder uniting heaven and earth, an experience that he considered tantamount to coming to the house of God, to the very gate of heaven.

The house of God is a place of ascent and descent. God descends to man, and man ascends to God. The ladder signified the notion of Jacob drawing near to his creator. We can imagine both the thrill and the fear of such an awesome experience. Such a uniting of heaven and earth pointed forward to what God would do through the Lord Jesus Christ.

While we might use a variety of words to describe the role that Jesus occupies on behalf of sinners, we need to add the word "ladder" to the list. Near the beginning of Jesus' public ministry, Philip told Nathanael that they had found the Christ which Moses and the prophets wrote about (John 1:45). Nathanael was skeptical about this claim at first, until he spoke with Jesus himself (1:46-49). Nathanael told Jesus, "Rabbi, you are the Son of God! You are the King of Israel!" (1:49). Jesus responded to Nathanael by invoking language from Genesis 28.

The Ladder Uniting Heaven and Earth

He said, "Truly, truly, I say to you, you will see heaven opened, and the angels of God ascending and descending on the Son of Man" (John 1:51). In Genesis 28:12, the angels were ascending and descending on the ladder. In John 1:51, Jesus says the angels will be ascending and descending on the Son of Man. The ladder that unites heaven and earth in Genesis 28 is a type of Christ, for the Lord Jesus is the one who goes to earth. He is the incarnate one and the reconciler of sinners to God. Jesus is the incarnate gate of heaven. He is Bethel in the flesh. He is the ladder which descends.

The news in Genesis 11:1-9 is that man cannot build a connection between earth and heaven in order to ascend to God. But the news in Genesis 28:10-17 is that God can come to humanity. The good news of Christ's birth is that the Lord has come to us. When the shepherds left the manger and returned to their fields after witnessing the newborn Christ, each of them could have the words of Jacob on their lips: "Surely the Lord is in this place, and I did not know it" (Gen. 28:16).

10

The Humiliation and Exaltation of Joseph

With his four wives, Jacob had twelve sons, and one son saved them all. The family's dilemma arose in Genesis 41, when a famine spread through many lands and affected Canaan (Gen. 41:54). And the reason why Joseph could rescue his family was because of an earlier tragedy that his brothers meant for evil.

Having actual dreams of future power and being the favored son of his father, Jacob, young Joseph experienced the hostility and opposition of his brothers (Gen. 37:3-11). When they had an opportune moment to rid themselves of Joseph, they took it. They cast him into a pit, a cistern (37:22-24). Soon afterward, they sold him to traders for pieces of silver, and the traders took him to Egypt (37:28). When the brothers returned to their

The Humiliation and Exaltation of Joseph

father Jacob, they deceived him by letting him think Joseph had been killed by a wild animal (37:31-33).

Unbeknownst to those conniving brothers, Joseph's life in Egypt would take stunning turns. He became a servant in Potiphar's home, until Potiphar's wife falsely accused Joseph of assault when he refused her sexual advances (Gen. 39:7-14). Potiphar's response led to Joseph's imprisonment (39:20). But even in prison, the Lord's hand was with Joseph, setting him apart and preparing him for what was to come. To this point, the biblical author narrated Joseph's humiliation. He went into a pit, down into Egypt, into servitude at Potiphar's home, and then into prison. Joseph had been brought low indeed. And now the Lord would raise him up.

Pharaoh learned that Joseph had interpreted the dream of a prisoner (Gen. 41:9-13), and Pharaoh needed his own dreams explained. So he summoned Joseph and heard the interpretation (41:25-36). A famine was coming, but Egypt had time to prepare. In a remarkable twist of circumstances and status, Joseph was appointed second-in-command over Egypt (41:39-43). Because of Joseph's new role, he would be in a position to deliver those who came to him for grain during the famine.

One day, Joseph's brothers arrived on his doorstep, though they didn't recognize him (Gen. 42:5-7). After a series of tests for his brothers, to see if they had changed, Joseph eventually made himself known to them, and they were reconciled in a scene of great weeping and compassion (45:1-15). Joseph explained to them, "And now do not be distressed or angry with yourselves because you sold me here, for God sent me before you to preserve life" (45:5). He rightly discerned the hand of God working providentially through the Egyptian captivity he faced. He told his brothers to retrieve their families from Canaan and to return to Egypt, specifically to the land of Goshen, where

The Humiliation and Exaltation of Joseph

Joseph could ensure their well-being and flourishing (45:9-13). So to Goshen the Israelites traveled, and Jacob reunited with his son whom he thought was long gone and dead (Gen. 46-47). Through Joseph's provision and the new location, the Israelites flourished under God's blessing (47:27).

Near the end of Joseph's life, his father gathered the sons for a blessing. And Joseph heard his father speak words about Judah: "The scepter shall not depart from Judah, nor the ruler's staff from between his feet, until tribute comes to him; and to him shall be the obedience of the peoples. Binding his foal to the vine and his donkey's colt to the choice vine, he has washed his garments in wine and his vesture in the blood of grapes" (Gen. 49:10–11).

The tribe of Judah would be the tribe from which a ruler would arise. Though Joseph had great authority and rule in Egypt, there was a future Israelite who would receive tribute and obedience. Joseph was a type of this future king, this Christ. The future ruler would be greatly blessed, with abundant vineyards and pleasant features (Gen. 49:11-12). A day would come, indeed, when Israel's king would ride a donkey that had been tied and kept ready (Gen. 49:11; Matt. 21:2-3). He would hold the scepter—a symbol of his rule.

But this future king's exaltation would be through the path of humiliation. Jesus, like Joseph, was rejected by his brothers. They thought, "He is out of his mind" (Mark 3:21). They did not believe in him until after his resurrection (John 7:5; Acts 1:14). Not only did Jesus face the unbelief of his household brothers, he faced rejection from his Jewish kinsmen. John's Gospel reports the heartbreaking news: "He came to his own, and his own people did not receive him" (John 1:11).

Jesus' kinsmen conspired against him, plotting his demise and death, especially when they discerned that he presented himself

The Humiliation and Exaltation of Joseph

as their Messiah and as someone sent from the Father. Joseph had been sold for silver, and Judas made a deal with the religious leaders to betray Jesus to them for pieces of silver (Gen. 37:28; Matt. 26:14-16). Jesus faced the false accusations of those who were determined to bring him down (Mark 14:55-56).

The humiliation of Jesus climaxed at his death on the cross. Flogged and bleeding, suffering and disgraced, he was raised up on the rugged wood (John 19:1, 16-18). But God raised his Son from death, installing him as the forever-king from the tribe of Judah. This is the pattern of humiliation and exaltation, a pattern evident in multiple Old Testament characters—like Joseph.

Paul drew attention to this pattern when he said that Jesus, "though he was in the form of God, did not count equality with God a thing to be grasped, but emptied himself, by taking the form of a servant, being born in the likeness of men. And being found in human form, he humbled himself by becoming obedient to the point of death, even death on a cross. Therefore God has exalted him and bestowed on him the name that is above every name, so that at the name of Jesus every knee should bow, in heaven and on earth and under the earth, and every tongue confess that Jesus Christ is Lord, to the glory of God the Father" (Phil. 2:6-11).

Rejected and humiliated and killed, Jesus rose and ascended in victory and glory. All authority belongs to him. What others meant for evil against him, God meant for good. The incarnation was for salvation—*our* salvation. He was born to rule. Jesus told Pilate, "You say that I am a king. For this purpose I was born and for this purpose I have come into the world" (John 18:37).

11

Moses, the Rejected Prophet and Deliverer

The person of Moses looms like a large shadow over the books of Exodus, Leviticus, Numbers, and Deuteronomy. It is hard to understate the importance of his prophetic ministry and leadership for the people of Israel. A clue that Moses would be an important figure for the Israelites is given when we read the story of his birth. We don't have birth reports for most Old Testament people. So when we do see a birth account, we should lean forward with even greater interest to see what happens next.

The context for Moses' birth was Israel's subjection to Egyptian slavery. The people of God were a captive people, harshly treated and oppressed. The wicked pharaoh was afraid of the multiplying Israelites, so he ordered that male Hebrew babies be killed. He told midwives to kill them (Exod. 1:16),

Moses, the Rejected Prophet and Deliverer

but when that didn't seem effective, he ordered that they be cast into the Nile River (1:22).

There was a Hebrew mother who conceived and bore a son, and she concealed her baby boy for several months (Exod. 2:1-2). Finally, she took him to the bank of the Nile River and, placing him in a small basket, set him strategically among the reeds (2:3). Pharaoh's daughter discovered him and, in God's providence, decided to adopt him (2:5-6). She needed a woman to nurse him until he could be weaned, and the child's own mother (2:7) fulfilled this role (2:8-9). When the child grew older, he was taken into pharaoh's home and became pharaoh's daughter's son. She named him Moses, "Because I drew him out of the water" (Exod. 2:10).

God protected Moses from the evil pharaoh's wicked scheme. As an adult, Moses rescued a Hebrew from being beaten by an Egyptian, but he was rejected by some of his own people (Exod. 2:14). When Pharaoh learned what Moses had done, Moses fled Egypt and stayed in the land of Midian (2:11-22). But his departure from Egypt was not permanent. He would return, and the next time he left, he would have a nation behind him.

At age eighty, Moses encountered the Lord's voice at a strangely burning bush on Mount Sinai. And God told him to go to pharaoh: "Come, I will send you to Pharaoh that you may bring my people, the children of Israel, out of Egypt" (Exod. 3:10). The Israelites initially struggled to embrace Moses (5:20-21). Nevertheless, the mighty Pharaoh and the fearful Israelites would not prevent God's plan of rescue. Through signs and wonders, God demonstrated divine supremacy and authority over Egypt and its many gods. Not even the great Pharaoh could stay Yahweh's hand.

Ten plagues unfolded as God brought judgment upon the land of Egypt and the king's administration (Exod. 7–12). And

Moses, the Rejected Prophet and Deliverer

Moses led the people out of captivity and toward the Promised Land. This departure was the famous "exodus." Moses was the deliverer whom God raised up to lead the exodus from Egypt. He was born to rescue them. Not only did he lead them out of Egypt, he also led them through the Red Sea when God made the water stand up like walls (Exod. 14).

Moses' leadership for the Israelites continued after their deliverance. He led them into the wilderness and to Mount Sinai. He served as a prophetic voice, declaring the words of God to the people of God. But the fearful and finicky people were ready to reject Moses and follow a new leader *back to Egypt* (Num. 14:1-4). When the Lord pronounced a forty-year judgment on the rebellious wilderness generation, Moses led the people for those decades as well. The book of Deuteronomy reports the last stage of Moses' life as the people of Israel were on the east side of the Jordan River and positioned to enter the Promised Land.

Among his sermons to the new generation of Israelites, Moses said, "The Lord your God will raise up for you a prophet like me from among you, from your brothers—it is to him you shall listen" (Deut. 18:15). God told Moses, "I will raise up for them a prophet like you from among their brothers. And I will put my words in his mouth, and he shall speak to them all that I command him" (18:18).

The "prophet like Moses" was the Lord Jesus. When the first-century generation heard Jesus speak, they were hearing the words of God. He ministered to a generation, however, that rejected him (Matt. 11:20-24). He was born to rescue and redeem, but he faced the fearfulness and unbelief of many around him.

Matthew's Gospel reports how early the opposition against Jesus started. Herod the Great wanted to kill the newborn

Moses, the Rejected Prophet and Deliverer

child, so he commissioned soldiers to kill the male children in Bethlehem (Matt. 2:13-18). Jesus was a new Moses who was under threat from a new Pharaoh. And, as was the case with Moses, Jesus was spared from death, despite the wicked plots of Herod the Great (2:14-15).

Jesus was the promised prophet and the ultimate rescuer. He came to lead a greater exodus than his ancient predecessor. This truth was especially clear when Jesus transfigured before some of his disciples on a mountain, and Moses and Elijah appeared and spoke with him (Luke 9:28-30). Moses and Elijah "spoke of his departure, which he was about to accomplish at Jerusalem" (9:31). The word for "departure" is the same word for "exodus." Jesus was going to accomplish an *exodus*. But from what? Not from Egyptian captivity. His greater exodus would be from a greater plight. Jesus came to rescue us from sin and death and judgment.

Moses had shepherded sheep in Midian for forty years, and then went on to shepherd people for forty years. Jesus was the good shepherd and faithful leader who presided over his flock. He led them and nourished them. He protected them and taught them; he laid his life down for their sake (John 10:14-15). He was born to redeem sinners from the captivity of their transgressions. He came to proclaim liberty.

Christ's greater work was marked by even greater glory than Moses. The writer of Hebrews said, "For Jesus has been counted worthy of more glory than Moses—as much more glory as the builder of a house has more honor than the house itself" (Heb. 3:3). Moses was faithful "as a servant," but Christ Jesus was faithful "as a son" (3:5-6). In the fullness of time, this son was born to speak the words of God and redeem a people for God.

12

The Unblemished Lamb

A series of divine judgments left Egypt in a destitute condition. Starting with the Nile River turning to blood, the plagues were a demonstration of Yahweh's supremacy over the Egyptian pantheon and their Pharaoh. The tenth and final plague would be devastating: "About midnight I will go out in the midst of Egypt, and every firstborn in the land of Egypt shall die, from the firstborn of Pharaoh who sits on his throne, even to the firstborn of the slave girl who is behind the handmill, and all the firstborn of the cattle" (Exod. 11:4-5).

But God would spare the Israelites from this plague upon the firstborn sons if they followed instructions about a sacrifice. They needed to take a lamb without blemish, kill it, and put its blood on the doorposts and lintel of their homes (Exod. 12:5-7). Blood would be on the outside of the home, and feasting would be on the inside. They would eat the meat of the lamb, along with unleavened bread and bitter

The Unblemished Lamb

herbs (12:8). And they were to eat this meal with an unusual readiness: "with your belt fastened, your sandals on your feet, and your staff in your hand. And you shall eat it in haste. It is the Lord's Passover" (12:11).

The need to eat in haste was because of the imminent exodus. Moses wanted the Israelites to be ready, so he called the Israelite leaders together and said, "Go and select lambs for yourselves according to your clans, and kill the Passover lamb. Take a bunch of hyssop and dip it in the blood that is in the basin, and touch the lintel and the two doorposts with the blood that is in the basin. None of you shall go out of the door of his house until the morning. For the Lord will pass through to strike the Egyptians, and when he sees the blood on the lintel and on the two doorposts, the Lord will pass over the door and will not allow the destroyer to enter your houses to strike you" (Exod. 12:21-23).

The Israelites heeded the words of Moses (Exod. 12:28). Then midnight arrived, and the Lord struck down the firstborn throughout the land of Egypt (12:29). A great cry filled the land (12:30). The Egyptians feared that the firstborn was the beginning of deaths—"We shall all be dead," they feared (12:33). Pharaoh and the Egyptians urged the Israelites out of the land. So that very day, the exodus took place (12:50-51).

The sacrifice of the unblemished lamb inaugurated the first of the festivals for Israel's calendar year. In the first month of the year, the Israelites would mark Passover and remember the rescuing hand of Yahweh (Exod. 12:2; 13:4-10). Year by year they were to keep the feast and remember what God had done (13:9-10).

In God's plan, the Passover foreshadowed what Jesus had come to do. As he grew up in Nazareth, he attended the annual feasts that were part of the Hebrew calendar, and he continued

The Unblemished Lamb

this rhythm during his earthly ministry (see, for example, Luke 2:41; John 2:13; 5:1; 7:1-10; 10:22). In fact, so important was the Hebrew calendar for Christ that it is associated with his death on the cross.

Jesus died not just on any day or on any month of the year. He died *on Passover*. During the meal leading to this ordained crucifixion, Jesus sat with his disciples and, as the host of the meal, would be expected to lead the ceremonial language and remembrance of the exodus. But the Last Supper wasn't like any other Passover meal his disciples had ever attended. Rather than attending to the elements of the meal and invoking the exodus, he referred to the bread and the cup and associated them with himself. Rather than speaking about what Moses and Israel had experienced, Jesus spoke about what he was going to do.

Breaking the bread, Jesus said, "Take; this is my body" (Mark 14:22). Taking the cup, he said, "This is my blood of the covenant, which is poured out for many" (14:24). Since Jesus' mission could be described as a new exodus, his disciples would naturally recall the importance of the unblemished lamb in Exodus 12 and wonder about the new and corresponding sacrifice. And, indeed, there was an unblemished lamb with the disciples at the table. Jesus was this lamb.

Paul told the Corinthians, "Christ, our Passover lamb, has been sacrificed" (1 Cor. 5:7). An unblemished offering meant an offering without defect. There was no defect in the Lord Jesus Christ. He was without sin. He was an unblemished lamb. Pilate himself confirmed this on the Friday of Jesus' crucifixion. Pilate said, "You brought me this man as one who was misleading the people. And after examining him before you, behold, I did not find this man guilty of any of your charges against him. Neither did Herod, for he sent him back to us. Look, nothing deserving death has been done by him" (Luke 23:14-15).

The Unblemished Lamb

Pilate was not sending a guilty man to the cross. An unblemished lamb was being offered. Jesus was "without sin" (Heb. 4:15) so that he might become sin for us (2 Cor. 5:21). Jesus died as our perfect Passover sacrifice. And just as in the book of Exodus, all who are covered by the shed blood of Christ will be delivered from the judgment of God.

One glory of the Son's incarnation was his human innocence, his purity. He possessed a human nature uncorrupted and unmarred by sin. Mary held in her arms the Lamb of God wrapped in swaddling cloths. For any who beheld the newborn Christ and had the spiritual sight to announce what God had given his people, they could say what would eventually be uttered by John: "Behold, the Lamb of God, who takes away the sin of the world!" (John 1:29).

13

Israel, the Firstborn Son

When you think of the Israelites in the Old Testament, what kind of descriptors would you use for them? They are a people; they are a nation; they are descendants of Abraham. All of that is true. Have you considered that God calls the Israelites his son? The nation of Israel in the Old Testament is the corporate son of God.

Moses had the nerve-wracking task of going into the presence of Egypt's king and demanding that the king let the Israelites go free. God said to Moses, "You shall say to Pharaoh, 'Thus says the Lord, Israel is my firstborn son, and I say to you, "Let my son go that he may serve me." If you refuse to let him go, behold, I will kill your firstborn son'" (Exod. 4:22-23). In other words, the firstborn sons of Egypt were in danger if Pharaoh didn't release God's firstborn son—the Israelites.

Israel's sonship was a collective, or corporate, reality. God called his son out of Egypt, for the Israelites left the land of

Israel, the Firstborn Son

captivity through the epic exodus which Moses led. These twelve tribes trekked through the wilderness to Mount Sinai, where God delivered his law through his servant Moses. This mountain became a place of divine revelation and communion. But Mount Sinai was not the goal of their exodus. The Israelites followed Moses from Sinai and traveled toward Canaan.

These Israelites traveled into the wilderness, where they faced various trials and temptations. The people murmured against the Lord, claiming that they had it better in Egypt than in the wilderness. They even called for a new leader who would rise up and deliver them from the accursed wilderness journey.

The story of Israel in the wilderness, then, was a story of a disobedient son. Though called to keep God's commands, they turned from his commands. Though summoned to fear the Lord and serve him only, they were entranced by other religious practices and the allurement of idols. God's son, Israel, acted rebelliously and faced a forty-year judgment, during which time the older generation of rebel Israelites would perish in the wilderness.

God had redeemed and covenanted with the Israelites. They were his people, his corporate child, and he guided and sustained the nation through the wilderness wandering. Under Joshua's leadership, God's son received the promised inheritance—the land of Canaan. The nation went through the Jordan River and received victory over enemies. Afterward, the Israelites dispersed into their various allotments which God had assigned them.

Subsequent years demonstrated, however, that their victories in Canaan would not sustain a people who were inwardly defiant against the Lord. The nation could not keep the Sinai Covenant. They engaged in such blatant and blasphemous activities that God's prophets warned of the covenant curses,

62

Israel, the Firstborn Son

which would culminate in exile from the Promised Land. Sure enough, the days of destruction came. God raised up foreign adversaries—the Assyrians and later the Babylonians—as rods of divine judgment. And God's son was expelled from the land, like an exile from Eden all over again. Israel was like a corporate Adam, who fell into into disobedience because they did not keep the revealed words of their God.

If we keep the notion of Israel's sonship in our minds, it will illuminate the Gospel stories of Jesus' earthly ministry. Israel in the Old Testament was a type of Christ in the New. Jesus was the incarnate and obedient Son of God. Though Israel had not been faithful, Jesus would be faithful. He would be the obedient Son who overcame temptation and who fulfilled the divine commandments. Jesus was a greater Israel, the *true* Israel. The nation had been like a "vine out of Egypt," which the Lord had redeemed and then planted in the Promised Land (Ps. 80:8). But in one of his famous "I Am" sayings, Jesus said, "I am the true vine" (John 15:1).

We need to think about Israel in the Old Testament when we read the stories of Jesus in the New. When Jesus was a baby and Joseph took him and Mary to Egypt, Matthew tells us that this was to "fulfill what the Lord had spoken by the prophet, 'Out of Egypt I called my son'" (Matt. 2:15, quoting Hosea. 11:1). The quotation from Hosea 11:1 was about God's son Israel, but because Israel was a type of Christ, Hosea 11:1 was also relevant to—and even fulfilled by—Christ in his earthly ministry. Jesus is the true and greater Israel.

How many disciples did Jesus call to himself? Twelve—the same number as the tribes of Israel. In Matthew's Gospel, Jesus went into the waters of the Jordan River (Matt. 3:13-17), and when Jesus emerged from his baptism, a voice from heaven said, "This is my beloved Son, with whom I am well pleased" (3:17).

63

Israel, the Firstborn Son

Going into the Jordan River recalled the background of the nation which had been poised to receive their Promised Land.

Jesus went into the wilderness, like the Israelites did, and faced temptation. They were in the wilderness for a period of forty (years), and Jesus was in the wilderness for a period of forty (days). The devil himself came to Christ with snares to set (Matt. 4:1-11). Jesus responded with Scripture, quoting from Deuteronomy in particular, and quoting from places which connected to Israel's wilderness experience and failures. Yet where Israel had failed, Jesus was faithful. He was the obedient Son who overcame the tempter and evaded the snares.

In Matthew 5–7, Jesus went to a mountain and spoke of God's law. But unlike Israel, which had broken God's commands, Jesus had come to fulfill them (Matt. 5:17). Jesus was and is the eternally begotten Son of God, and at the incarnation he took to himself a truly human nature without negating or undermining his divine nature. On the one hand, we can appropriately think of Jesus as the eternal Son of God. And on the other hand, we can appropriately think of Jesus as the true Israel whom God brought into the world to be the obedient and faithful Son.

As the one who perfectly kept the law, Christ could redeem us from the curse of the law by satisfactorily bearing that curse in our place.

14

Bread from Heaven

As a faithful Father, the Lord watched over and provided for his people as they journeyed through the wilderness between Egypt and the Promised Land. But some episodes recounted the doubts of the Israelites that God would always be so attentive and giving.

For example, when the Israelites were several weeks into their trip, the whole congregation grumbled against Moses and Aaron in the wilderness (Exod. 16:1-2). The Israelites said to them, "Would that we had died by the hand of the Lord in the land of Egypt, when we sat by the meat pots and ate bread to the full, for you have brought us out into this wilderness to kill this whole assembly with hunger" (16:3).

But, of course, the Lord had not brought them into the wilderness to kill them. Though they had panicked and spoken with despair, the Lord would provide miraculously for them.

Bread from Heaven

He said, "Behold, I am about to rain bread from heaven for you, and the people shall go out and gather a day's portion every day, that I may test them, whether they will walk in my law or not. On the sixth day, when they prepare what they bring in, it will be twice as much as they gather daily" (Exod. 16:4-5).

The Lord's announcement was about the provision of what became known as *manna*. The biblical author said, "It was like coriander seed, white, and the taste of it was like wafers made with honey" (Exod. 16:31). This manna, this bread substance, was God's heavenly gift to them each morning. They would emerge from their tents, and there they would find the provision of the Lord—except on the seventh day. God prohibited a gathering of bread on the seventh day, so he provided twice as much on the sixth day. This sixth-day gathering would ensure that no seventh-day gathering would be necessary.

So important was this manna that Moses said, "This is what the Lord has commanded: 'Let an omer of it be kept throughout your generations, so that they may see the bread with which I fed you in the wilderness, when I brought you out of the land of Egypt'" (Exod. 16:32). Eventually this jar of manna would be kept with the ark of the covenant behind the veil of the tabernacle.

How faithful was God's provision of manna for his people? "The people of Israel ate the manna forty years, till they came to a habitable land. They ate the manna till they came to the border of the land of Canaan" (Exod. 16:35). The book of Joshua reports the ceasing of the manna: "And the day after the Passover, on that very day, they ate of the produce of the land, unleavened cakes and parched gain. And the manna ceased the day after they ate of the produce of the land. And there was no longer any manna for the people of Israel, but they ate of the fruit of the land of Canaan that year" (Josh. 5:11-12).

Bread from Heaven

For forty years the Lord provided enough manna for every day of the week. The Israelites woke up every morning to a miracle. And yet the temporariness of the provision was evident in the fact that they had to gather the food daily. Its temporariness was also evident in the fact that it lasted until they were in the Promised Land. The nature of the manna was typological, forward-pointing, like a sign of something that would actually last and deeply satisfy. Better bread was on the way.

One of Jesus' most famous miracles was the feeding of the five thousand, and in John's Gospel, we learn that this miracle was the occasion for a lengthier teaching about bread and Jesus' identity. From five loaves and two fish, Jesus fed thousands of people (John 6:9-11). There was even food left over, enough for twelve baskets filled with bread (6:12-13).

When people came to him the next day, he told them, "Truly, truly, I say to you, you are seeking me, not because you saw signs, but because you ate your fill of the loaves. Do not work for the food that perishes, but for the food that endures to eternal life, which the Son of Man will give to you" (John 6:26-27). Here, Jesus distinguishes between food that perishes and food that doesn't.

Jesus said, "Truly, truly, I say to you, it was not Moses who gave you the bread from heaven, but my Father gives you the true bread from heaven. For the bread of God is he who comes down from heaven and gives life to the world" (John 6:32-33).

The people asked for this bread (John 6:34). But they didn't realize that this bread is right in front of them. Jesus said, "I am the bread of life; whoever comes to me shall not hunger, and whoever believes in me shall never thirst" (6:35). He is the bread of heaven. The incarnation was the heavenly descent of everlasting bread. He said, "I am the bread that came down from heaven" (6:41). This claim was confusing to them. They

Bread from Heaven

asked, "Is not this Jesus, the son of Joseph, whose father and mother we know? How does he now say, 'I have come down from heaven'?" (6:42).

Though they saw Jesus face to face, they did not recognize everything that was true about him. However, he didn't back away from his claim. "Truly, truly, I say to you, whoever believes has eternal life. I am the bread of life. Your fathers ate the manna in the wilderness, and they died. This is the bread that comes down from heaven, so that one may eat of it and not die. I am the living bread that came down from heaven. If anyone eats of this bread, he will live forever. And the bread that I will give for the life of the world is my flesh" (John 6:47-51).

The crowd didn't understand everything Jesus taught that day. But their lack of perception didn't negate the objective truth about who Jesus was and what he had come to do. He had come to give life, *eternal* life. He was and is better manna because he was and is *everlasting* bread. He gives life not to Israelites in the wilderness but to sinners throughout the world. When he spoke of his body at the Last Supper, he did so while holding bread: "And as they were eating, he took bread, and after blessing it broke it and gave it to them, and said, 'Take; this is my body'" (Mark 14:22).

As the bread of heaven, Jesus would be given to us and broken for us.

15

Water from the Rock

Our bodies need food and water, and God provided both to the Israelites in the wilderness. And there were times he did so in a miraculous manner. Beginning in Exodus 16, the people received daily manna from the Lord. Though they murmured against Moses and ultimately against the Lord, they experienced the provision of the Lord, day by day.

In Exodus 17, the issue of water was in the foreground. Not seeing any water where they camped, the people told Moses, "Give us water to drink," and they did this with a quarrelsome spirit (Exod. 17:1-2). The situation escalated when they asked, "Why did you bring us up out of Egypt, to kill us and our children and our livestock with thirst?" (17:3). This panic and complaint come after the miracle of manna. But rather than trusting that the Lord would provide water for their thirst, the people complained against Moses.

Water from the Rock

God would once again display his power. He told Moses, "Pass on before the people, taking with you some of the elders of Israel, and take in your hand the staff with which you struck the Nile, and go. Behold, I will stand before you there on the rock at Horeb, and you shall strike the rock, and water shall come out of it, and the people will drink" (Exod. 17:5-6).

Moses obeyed the Lord (Exod. 17:6). The whole process, though, must have seemed strange. A strike with the staff from the plague episodes? A rock pouring forth water? And, perhaps just as strange, if not more so, the Lord would be upon the rock when Moses struck it.

Thinking through these elements of the scene, consider the role of the staff. The staff in Exodus 7–12 symbolized God's authority as he brought judgments upon the land of Egypt. Whether Moses held the staff or whether Aaron did, the Lord's authority was the point. And now, in Exodus 17, Moses would take this same staff and strike a rock upon which the Lord was standing. Can you imagine Moses thinking, "Lord, if you are upon the rock and I'm supposed to strike it, won't you receive the strike from the staff?"

Picture it: the Lord tells Moses to strike the rock, and the Lord will—so to speak—be struck by this staff. It's a picture of the Lord taking the judgment for the people and, through this judgment, providing deliverance for them. In Exodus 17, the water flows when the rock is struck. The staff of judgment is simultaneously the staff of deliverance.

Though the struck rock displayed the miraculous power of the Lord, the water was normal water. Water from this rock would not quench the people's thirst eternally. They would be thirsty again. But in the giving of this water from the rock, the Lord was foreshadowing the lasting life that he would give to sinners through his Son.

Water from the Rock

To a Samaritan woman at a well, Jesus referred to himself as the source of something greater than earthly water. He told her, "If you knew the gift of God, and who it is that is saying to you, 'Give me a drink,' you would have asked him, and he would have given you living water" (John 4:10).

Understandably, the woman inquired about this living water, but she was still thinking of the well where they were having this conversation. Jesus told her, "Everyone who drinks of this water will be thirsty again, but whoever drinks of the water that I will give him will never be thirsty again. The water that I will give him will become in him a spring of water welling up to eternal life" (John 4:13-14).

Not only is Jesus the bread of life, he is the water of life. He said, "Whoever comes to me shall not hunger, and whoever believes in me shall never thirst" (John 6:35). The thirsty soul finds its satisfaction in Christ alone. All other sources cannot quench it. All other waters fail to satisfy.

Consider, again, the picture of the object (the rock) being struck (by the staff) in order to meet the people's need (thirst). Now consider how that pattern is christological. The rock foreshadows the Messiah who will be struck. Through his suffering and death on the cross, lifegiving mercy flows to sinners. Paul told the Corinthians that "the Rock was Christ" (1 Cor. 10:4).

Christ is the lifegiving rock of ages. Living water flows from him for all who come to him to drink. And when they trust him, their heart has found its resting place in him. The truth of Christ's efficacy is grounded in who he is and what he has done. As the Son of God, he is the eternal source of life. Indeed, there is no lasting life apart from him. And by virtue of his death on the cross, he has received the "striking" of divine judgment. He bore the wrath of God in our place. And because he rose from

Water from the Rock

the dead, he is not a dried up source; he is the living source of living water. He is not a rock for a mere region or a well for a generation. He is the heavenly rock of eternal life for all peoples and at all times and in all places.

The incarnation is God's provision for his spiritually thirsty people. The Son of God becomes flesh and is born for our eternal satisfaction—our eternal *life*. Whoever believes in him will not thirst. So the prophet says, "Come, everyone who thirsts, come to the waters; and he who has no money, come, buy and eat! Come, buy wine and milk without money and without price" (Isa. 55:1).

16

Immanuel and the Tabernacle

The Israelites did not travel alone. As Moses led them, the Lord was with them and guided them. We see a description of this in Exodus 13, after the exodus from Egypt: "And the LORD went before them by day in a pillar of cloud to lead them along the way, and by night in a pillar of fire to give them light, that they might travel by day and by night. The pillar of cloud by day and the pillar of fire by night did not depart from before the people" (Exod. 13:21-22).

The Lord led the Israelites through the Red Sea and toward Mount Sinai. They arrived at Mount Sinai in Exodus 19, and they left it in Numbers 10. The Lord's presence with the people was evident when he descended upon the mountain in a fearsome theophany, with smoke and fire and thunder (Exod. 19:16-20). God's revelation to the people consisted of what we know as the Ten Commandments (20:1-17). And then subsequent revelation came through Moses, their mediator.

73

Immanuel and the Tabernacle

Part of this revelation included instructions to build a portable tent, a dwelling place that would be known as the tabernacle or the tent of meeting.

The tabernacle consisted of two rooms, one large room called the Holy Place and a smaller cube-shaped room called the Most Holy Place. Each of these rooms contained special furniture. Outside these two rooms of the tabernacle, there was a courtyard, and outside the courtyard was the camp of Israel. The courtyard entrance was on the east side, and right inside the courtyard was a bronze altar on which the priests offered the appropriate sacrifices (Lev. 1–7). Passing by the sacrificial altar and heading west toward the Holy Place, there stood a bronze basin where priests would wash their hands and feet.

Inside the tabernacle's Holy Place were three pieces of furniture. Along the north wall was a golden table of bread. It held twelve loaves that were stacked in two piles of six. The priests exchanged the old bread for fresh bread on the sabbath. It symbolized God's fellowship with his people. Opposite the table of bread, and along the south wall of the Holy Place, was a golden lampstand. It was also known as a menorah, and it lit the Holy Place and shined upon the table of bread. The menorah, with all of its branches and oil and fire, symbolized the truth that God was the light of his people. On the west side of the Holy Place and in front of a veil, there was a golden altar of incense, which symbolized the prayers and intercession of God's people, who were represented by the priests.

Behind the veil in the Holy Place was the Most Holy Place, a cube-shaped room accessible only once a year (on the Day of Atonement; see Lev. 16). This small room was covered by a veil in order to emphasize its holiness, its sacredness. This Most Holy Place (or Holy of Holies) contained the ark of the covenant, which was a wooden box overlaid with gold. The ark's

Immanuel and the Tabernacle

lid—known as the mercy seat—was made of gold and had, on the top, two golden cherubim. Upon the ark and behind the veil, the glory of God manifested and rested.

The tabernacle rooms and furniture were integral to Israel's sacrificial system. Priests ministered at the tabernacle: only priests could enter the Holy Place, and only the high priest could enter the Most Holy Place. Because the tabernacle was a portable tent, the Israelites traveled with it by tearing it down whenever they departed and then setting it up wherever they camped. The tabernacle represented the presence of God dwelling with the Israelites.

God was with them as they journeyed. As they walked, they would be able to say, "We are not alone, for God is with us," because they had the tabernacle and, in particular, the ark of the covenant. The tabernacle was the message of Immanuel, which means "God with us." The tabernacle would later be replaced by the temple, and the temple would eventually be destroyed by Babylon and then rebuilt. Though the tabernacle played a temporary role in Israel's life, it played an important role. Its priests, offerings, and furniture all contributed to truths about God's holiness, mercy, hospitality, and presence.

Have you ever thought about how the tabernacle points to the person and work of Christ? The Gospel of John evokes this portable tent when the author tells us, "And the Word became flesh and dwelt among us, and we have seen his glory, glory as of the only Son from the Father, full of grace and truth" (John 1:14). The word "dwelt" means "tabernacled." The Word became flesh and *tabernacled* among us.

The birth of Jesus was better than the tabernacle's construction and operation. Jesus is Immanuel—"God with us" (Matt. 1:22-23). He is the tabernacling presence of God, dwelling with and ministering to sinners. The bronze altar

Immanuel and the Tabernacle

points to him, for he is the sacrifice that brings us near to God. The bronze basin of water points to him, for he is the one who cleanses sinners. The golden table of bread points to him, for he is everlasting bread. The golden lampstand points to him, for he is the light of the world. The golden altar of incense points to him, for he is the intercessor and mediator on behalf of sinners. The veil points to him, for his flesh is the veil that was torn for us that we might be reconciled to God. The ark points to him, for he is the fullness of deity dwelling under the sun.

The tabernacle was good news for the Israelites because it signaled that God had drawn near to sinners. He condescended. He stooped and dwelt. Even greater news is the incarnation of the Son, for God is with us in an even greater way. The tabernacle may have had an altar and an ark, but the Son of God has hands to receive us and a voice to welcome us.

17

The Staff of Aaron

Between Mount Sinai and the Promised Land, the Israelites had episodes of rebellion. A major rebellion took place in Numbers 13–14 when the people turned against Moses and were ready to return to Egypt under a new leader. For this egregious Israelite response, God pronounced a forty-year judgment upon the wilderness generation.

But the forty-year judgment didn't deter the hearts of rebels in every case. In Numbers 16, one of Moses' relatives caused a major issue that led to a catastrophic event. A man called Korah wasn't content with God's appointment of Aaron and Aaron's sons to be the priests. Korah insisted that "all in the congregation are holy, every one of them, and the Lord is among them" (Num. 16:3). Moses understood that Korah sought the priesthood (16:10). Even though Korah was a Levite, being from the tribe of Levi didn't seem sufficient. Korah wanted more, and his complaint was a manifestation of discontent and rebellion against the Lord. Moses told Korah and Korah's allies, "Therefore it is against the Lord that you and all your company have gathered together" (16:11).

The Staff of Aaron

Korah's rebellion led to a fearful judgment. Moses said, "If the Lord creates something new, and the ground opens its mouth and swallows them up with all that belongs to them, and they go down alive into Sheol, then you shall know that these men have despised the Lord" (Num. 16:30). Indeed, the ground opened. The earth swallowed Korah and his fellow rebels, along with all of their goods (16:31-33). This event confirmed what Moses had said: the rebels had despised the Lord, so they reaped judgment.

Not only did the Lord show that he had rejected Korah and the other rebels, he also publicly confirmed that Aaron and Aaron's line would be the priestly lineage. This confirmation involved Aaron's staff. God told Moses, "Speak to the people of Israel, and get from them staffs, one for each fathers' house, from all their chiefs according to their fathers' houses, twelve staffs. Write each man's name on his staff, and write Aaron's name on the staff of Levi. For there shall be one staff for the head of each fathers' house" (Num. 17:2-3).

Moses was then supposed to place the staffs in the tabernacle, and God would perform a wonder (Num. 17:4). He said, "The staff of the man whom I choose shall sprout. Thus I will make to cease from me the grumblings of the people of Israel, which they grumble against you" (17:5). The instructions were followed: staffs were collected, names were written, and the staffs were placed inside the tent of meeting (17:6-7). Importantly, the staff of Levi had Aaron's name on it.

The next day, Moses entered the tabernacle and retrieved Aaron's staff: "and behold, the staff of Aaron for the house of Levi had sprouted and put forth buds and produced blossoms, and it bore ripe almonds" (Num. 17:8). But no such wonder occurred for any of the other staffs. They were brought out and distributed back to the appropriate tribes (17:9).

The Staff of Aaron

God's decision was clear for all to see. The staff that sprouted was Aaron's and Aaron's alone. Levi was the chosen tribe for the priests, and the lineage would descend from their first high priest—Moses' older brother Aaron. The staff would remain in the Most Holy Place as a perpetual reminder of the chosen priestly line (Num. 17:10).

Such a miraculous confirmation of God's will was a shadow of what God would do in the ministry of Jesus. There were many Israelites, but only one Israelite would be the Messiah. There were many purported leaders of movements, but only one king could sustain a following that would rival empires and outlast all earthly kingdoms. The question was how someone might identify which man was the promised Son who would crush the serpent and deliver the captive?

Jesus was the chosen one. He said, "For the works that the Father has given me to accomplish, the very works that I am doing, bear witness about me that the Father has sent me" (John 5:36). In other words, Jesus' miracles were testifying to the truth about his identity: he is the Son of God. Consider, though, something more than the miracles Jesus performed for others. On the third day from his crucifixion, Jesus rose from the dead in victory.

If Jesus had remained dead, then he would have been like the mighty yet deceased leaders in Israel's history, some of whom were even miracle workers. Remember the greatness of Abraham and Moses, Joshua and David, Samson and Elisha. But their earthly greatness came to an end because of the grave. No matter what battles they fought, or what wonders were associated with them, or what reputation they garnered, they died and have stayed dead.

But the resurrection of Christ was like the staff of Aaron. Christ's bodily resurrection was a demonstration of who he was

The Staff of Aaron

and is: the Son of God and Messiah. Jesus is the Savior of sinners and the righteous judge of the wicked. How do we know this? Because he has risen from the dead. Paul told the Athenians, "The times of ignorance God overlooked, but now he commands all people everywhere to repent, because he has fixed a day on which he will judge the world in righteousness by a man whom he has appointed; and of this he has given assurance to all by raising him from the dead" (Acts 17:30-31).

The empty tomb echoes with the sound of assurance that Jesus is Lord and Savior. But what about something much earlier that might give assurance? Is there a heavenly demonstration early in the life of Jesus that he is the appointed Messiah and the Son of God? Consider the miracle of the incarnation. Only Aaron's staff budded and blossomed, so it was clear he was set apart by God. And only Jesus was born of a virgin. The angel told Mary, "And behold, you will conceive in your womb and bear a son, and you shall call his name Jesus. He will be great and will be called the Son of the Most High. And the Lord God will give to him the throne of his father David" (Luke 1:31-32).

Jesus was conceived because of a wonder; in his ministry he performed wonders, and his redeeming work was vindicated by the wonder of his resurrection. Greater than Aaron's staff, the incarnation of Jesus bloomed and blossomed with glory and power.

18

The Bronze Serpent

The most famous verse in the whole Bible might be John 3:16, and understandably so. The verse is a marvelous announcement of God's gracious work of provision as he gave his only Son for the salvation of sinners, a provision rooted in his divine love for the world.

But John 3:16, in context, is an explanation of a previous point. Jesus was explaining why people who believe in him will have eternal life (3:15). And that good news is pictured in the Old Testament with a story about a bronze serpent which Moses raised up in the wilderness for perishing people to see (3:14).

The story of the bronze serpent is in Numbers 21. The wilderness generation had wandered for decades, barred from the Promised Land until the last of their generation died. You would think that such judgment would deter future outbreaks of rebellion and moral insanity. But a familiar scene is noteworthy in Numbers 21:4, where "the people became impatient on the

The Bronze Serpent

way. And the people spoke against God and against Moses, 'Why have you brought us up out of Egypt to die in this wilderness? For there is no food and no water, and we loathe this worthless food'" (Num. 21:4-5).

In a horrifying turn of events, fiery serpents were sent among the Israelites, and they bit the people and caused many deaths (Num. 21:6). This was a judgment of God. Though not unjust, it was nevertheless severe. The terrifying situation prompted a penitent response as some Israelites went to Moses and said, "We have sinned, for we have spoken against the Lord and against you. Pray to the Lord, that he take away the serpents from us" (21:7).

Moses prayed for the people, and the Lord's response was a very specific instruction: "Make a fiery serpent and set it on a pole, and everyone who is bitten, when he sees it, shall live" (Num. 21:8). So Moses made a bronze serpent, raised it on a pole, and all who looked to it lived and did not perish (21:9).

The bronze serpent was God's provision for the perishing. The Israelites were bitten by fiery serpents, and a bronze serpent was the means of their deliverance. The dangerous serpents attacked the Israelites after the people had been brought up out of Egypt (Num. 21:5). Ancient pharaohs had a serpent on their headdress, and in Exodus 7:11-12, the staff of Moses became a serpent that ate up the other serpents.

Moses' staff that became a serpent in Exodus was a demonstration of Yahweh's supremacy and power over Pharaoh's magicians and Pharaoh himself. Furthermore, Yahweh was greater than all of Egypt's gods combined. In Numbers 21, Yahweh's supremacy is once again on display. A serpent defeats the serpents.

The pattern in Numbers 21 was God's provision of something that delivered the people, and that kind of pattern

82

The Bronze Serpent

is christological. Such a pattern is why Jesus speaks of his own future cross work in terms that recall the bronze serpent. In John 3:14-15 he says, "And as Moses lifted up the serpent in the wilderness, so must the Son of Man be lifted up, that whoever believes in him may have eternal life."

The escalation between the statements in Numbers 21 and John 3 is from physical death to spiritual death. The Israelites in the wilderness, who had been bitten by the poisonous serpents, could look at the bronze serpent and live. But according to Jesus' words, those who trust in him will not perish but have eternal life. The word "perish" isn't about physical death, for all die. The word must refer to *spiritual death*, and this meaning is confirmed by its opposite in the verse: *eternal life*.

While the bronze serpent could save the physically perishing, Jesus can save the spiritually perishing. And just as the bronze serpent was lifted up, the Son of Man would be lifted up. This "lifting up" imagery is fulfilled in the cross. Jesus, the Son of Man, was held high on the cross by the nails through his hands and feet. Lifted above the earth, the Lord Jesus satisfied the penalty for the poison of sin. All who trust in him are delivered from their malady. Though they die physically, they will live spiritually.

In John 3:14-15, we read Jesus' interpretation of the episode in Numbers 21:4-9. And his interpretation is typological. Because the cross of Jesus is the provision of God for the perishing, the earlier and temporary provisions are types which foreshadow Jesus. After saying that "whoever believes in him may have eternal life" (John 3:15), Jesus explains his claim in John 3:16: "For God so loved the world, that he gave his only Son, that whoever believes in him should not perish but have eternal life."

Before Christ was given for the world, he was given to the world. The incarnation was the birth of the promised Son,

The Bronze Serpent

who came because of divine love. The raising up of the bronze serpent was God's mercy displayed to a group of people in one region—the wilderness. The raising up of the cross was God's mercy displayed to all peoples and tribes and tongues around the world.

Long before Jesus was raised up on the cross, he was laid down in the manger. But the path was set, ordained from the foundation of the world. The baby in the manger would be the redeemer on the cross, so that all who look to him in faith would live.

19

The Zeal of Phinehas

The forty years of judgment on the wilderness generation was coming to an end. In the land of Moab, the Israelites were now east of the Jordan River. And they "began to whore with the daughters of Moab. These invited the people to the sacrifices of their gods, and the people ate and bowed down to their gods. So Israel yoked himself to Baal of Peor. And the anger of the LORD was kindled against Israel" (Num. 25:1-3).

Flagrant idolatry had taken place, and the Israelites were thoroughly involved in it. To make matters worse, the corresponding judgment was the most devastating one-time judgment that the Israelites faced in the Torah. By the time the unspecified plague on Israel ceased, approximately twenty-four thousand Israelites had perished (Num. 25:8-9).

But what brought about the end of this plague? The biblical author reports the zeal of a man named Phinehas. He was the son of Eleazar, and Eleazar was the son of Aaron. Because Aaron

The Zeal of Phinehas

died in Numbers 20:22-29, his son Eleazar was the current high priest, and that meant Phinehas was the son of the high priest and thus a priest.

Remembering Phinehas' actions is important for understanding why the plague on Israel ended. As one of the tabernacle's priests, Phinehas was charged with maintaining the sanctity of the sanctuary and protecting it from defilement. When "one of the people of Israel came and brought a Midianite woman to his family, in the sight of Moses and in the sight of the whole congregation of the people of Israel, while they were weeping in the entrance of the tent of meeting" (Num. 25:6), we learn that the subsequent outrageous act would be committed near the tabernacle.

Phinehas knew something wasn't right. He "rose and left the congregation and took a spear in his hand" (Num. 25:7). This weaponry was available to the Levites because of their charge to guard the tent of meeting. Provoked by their wickedness and animated with righteous indignation, Phinehas acted. He "went after the man of Israel into the chamber and pierced both of them, the man of Israel and the woman through her belly" (Num. 25:8). It was at this point that the plague ended.

In the middle of their sexual immorality, the couple perished. One spear pierced them both at the same time. This display of holy zeal stopped the rising death toll that was due to the plague (Num. 25:8-9). The Lord told Moses, "Phinehas the son of Eleazar, son of Aaron the priest, has turned back my wrath from the people of Israel, in that he was jealous with my jealousy among them, so that I did not consume the people of Israel in my jealousy" (25:11).

The wrath of God had rightly broken out against the sinning Israelites. And what Israel needed, in order to be spared, was for the wrath of God to be turned back. The act of Phinehas, spurred

The Zeal of Phinehas

on by his appropriate jealousy—or zeal—for the glory and holiness of God, turned back the righteous judgment of God.

Not only does the context of Numbers 25 portray Phinehas' zeal and response in a positive manner (Num. 25:7-11), a psalmist interprets the episode positively as well. We read that Israel "yoked themselves to the Baal of Peor, and ate sacrifices offered to the dead; they provoked the Lord to anger with their deeds, and a plague broke out among them. Then Phinehas stood up and intervened, and the plague was stayed. And that was counted to him as righteousness from generation to generation forever" (Ps. 106:28-31).

Phinehas acted by faith. He responded in Numbers 25 with a holy zeal and righteous anger. And his action with the spear brought an end to the plague because he turned back God's wrath from the people. Phinehas had been zealous for the Father's house, and the Father honored him for it.

No one had greater zeal for the glory of God and the holiness of God's house than Jesus. This truth was evident even when Jesus was a young boy. His parents found him at the Jerusalem temple when he was twelve years old, and he said, "Why were you looking for me? Did you not know that I must be in my Father's house?" (Luke 2:49). Zeal for the sanctuary was clear. But further evidence is clear in the Gospel of John.

As an adult in John 2:13-15, when the annual Passover was near, Jesus went to the Jerusalem temple and drove out money-changers and buyers and sellers who had turned the Father's house into a place of trade. He didn't carry a spear, but he made a whip of cords to accomplish the expulsion (2:15). His disciples later remembered what had been written: "Zeal for your house will consume me" (John 2:17, quoting Ps. 69:9).

Jesus was zealous for his Father's commands and his Father's house. He prioritized righteous activity and valued holy places.

The Zeal of Phinehas

His response at the temple in John 2 was like a Phinehas episode. But Jesus was a true and greater Phinehas. The plan of God was not for Jesus to administer the execution but for Jesus to stand in the place of the guilty. In Numbers 25, the righteous struck down the unrighteous. In the four Gospels, the righteous dies for the unrighteous. Jesus didn't throw a spear from his hand; he received a spear into his side: "But one of the soldiers pierced his side with a spear, and at once there came out blood and water" (John 19:34).

Greater than Phinehas, Jesus turned back the wrath of God by satisfying it. He averted it from others by bearing it himself. Though we deserved death and judgment for our sins and guilt, Christ has not dealt us the blow of death. Instead, he took the place of the guilty as the perfect substitute. He came into the world to turn back the righteous wrath of God.

20

The Saving Name of Joshua

Moses led the Israelites out of Egypt, but he wouldn't be the one to lead them into the Promised Land. He would die east of the Jordan River, at age 120. The new Moses was a man named Joshua, and he would lead the covenant people into their inheritance.

The first time we see Joshua's name is when the Israelites are under attack. In Exodus 17:8, the Amalekites fought against the Israelites at Rephidim. And Moses told Joshua, "Choose for us men, and go out and fight with Amalek. Tomorrow I will stand on the top of the hill with the staff of God in my hand" (Exod.17:9). Joshua obeyed Moses. He fought against the Amalekites, and Moses went to the top of the hill to raise the staff (17:10–12). Led by Joshua, the Israelites triumphed over their enemy (17:13).

Among the older generation of Israelites, only Joshua and Caleb would enter the Promised Land with the new generation

The Saving Name of Joshua

(see Num. 14:30). God told Moses that Joshua would be his successor: "Take Joshua the son of Nun, a man in whom is the Spirit, and lay your hand on him. Make him stand before Eleazar the priest and all the congregation, and you shall commission him in their sight. You shall invest him with some of your authority, that all the congregation of the people of Israel may obey" (Num. 27:18-20).

Joshua would be publicly recognized as, and commissioned to be, the new leader of Israel. The fulfillment of this instruction was reported in Deuteronomy 31. Moses, at 120 years old, was nearing death. He told the people, "The Lord your God himself will go over before you. He will destroy these nations before you, so that you shall dispossess them, and Joshua will go over at your head, as the Lord has spoken" (Deut. 31:3).

Moses summoned Joshua to appear before the Israelites and told him, "Be strong and courageous, for you shall go with this people into the land that the Lord has sworn to their fathers to give them, and you shall put them in possession of it. It is the Lord who goes before you. He will be with you; he will not leave you or forsake you. Do not fear or be dismayed" (Deut. 31:7-8). And the Lord's voice commissioned Joshua: "Be strong and courageous, for you shall bring the people of Israel into the land that I swore to give them. I will be with you" (31:23).

When his successor had been commissioned and installed, Moses died. (Deut. 34). Then the Lord called for Joshua to now lead the people of Israel across the Jordan River to receive the Promised Land (Josh. 1:1-3). He led them into battle, and the Lord gave them victory (Josh. 10–12).

One of the reasons it was fitting for Joshua to lead the people into their inheritance, and to have victory over their enemies, was his name. "Joshua" means "Yahweh is salvation." When we first met Joshua in Exodus 17:9, and he delivered the Israelites

The Saving Name of Joshua

from the Amalekites, Yahweh was bringing salvation through him. This deliverance was primarily in a corporate and military sense, as God advanced the dominion of the nation and subdued his enemies.

Greater deliverance was needed, however, because sinners face the shackles of their transgressions and the threat of condemnation for their guilt. And if greater deliverance was needed, then a greater Joshua was needed. Not only would Jesus be a greater Moses than Joshua was, he would also be greater than Joshua himself.

Though Joshua's birth wasn't prophesied, Jesus' birth was. The Old Testament predicted his coming, and the Gospels report the angelic announcement of an impending conception and birth. For example, Joseph, who was engaged to Mary, had a dream in which an angel appeared to him and said, "Joseph, son of David, do not fear to take Mary as your wife, for that which is conceived in her is from the Holy Spirit. She will bear a son, and you shall call his name Jesus, for he will save his people from their sins" (Matt. 1:20-21). The angel Gabriel told Mary the same thing: "Behold, you will conceive in your womb and bear a son, and you shall call his name Jesus" (Luke 1:31).

Significantly, not only did a heavenly pronouncement prophesy Jesus' birth, the angelic messengers also disclosed the child's name. The child would be named *Jesus*. The Greek for "Jesus" is the equivalent of the Hebrew for "Joshua." The name "Jesus" means "Yahweh is salvation." Jesus would live up to his name. He would provide salvation for people in the way that mattered most deeply. He would "save his people from their sins" (Matt. 1:21). The mission of Jesus is present in his very name.

Jesus, the greater Joshua, would lead his people into their inheritance as co-heirs. The Old Testament land of Canaan foreshadowed the new creation, and Jesus is leading his people

The Saving Name of Joshua

to this new creation. His work as a greater Joshua was already evident during his earthly ministry. He didn't face the embattled scenarios of Jericho and Ai. He triumphed, instead, over demons and disease and death. Like Joshua, Jesus traveled in the southern and northern parts of the land, yet Jesus' dominion over principalities and powers was a greater triumph than the Old Testament conquest. Jesus' conquest brought deliverance. He delivered the blind and the leper. He freed the demon-possessed. He opened the ears of the deaf and the mouths of the mute.

The conquest of the Christ left people restored and renewed and reconciled. For these reasons, there is no greater name than Jesus. At his name every knee should bow, and every tongue should confess him as Lord (Phil. 2:9-11). Peter proclaimed to the religious leaders, "There is salvation in no one else, for there is no other name under heaven given among men by which we must be saved" (Acts 4:12).

Joshua in the Old Testament accomplished victories and faithfully led his people. But the Joshua in the New Testament would save his people from their sins. His name—"Yahweh is salvation"—conveyed his mission in its syllables. When the promised child was born, Mary and Joseph did exactly what the angel had told them to do. They called his name Jesus (Matt. 1:25).

21

A Red Cord in the Window

In the years that followed the plagues upon Egypt and the destruction of the Egyptian soldiers in the Red Sea, word spread about Yahweh's victory and Israel's escape. Word of what happened even reached Canaan. And as the Israelites approached the Promised Land, ready for conquest, there were people in Canaan whose hearts filled with dread. Some inhabitants would resist the Israelites and combat them. Others were ready to trust Yahweh and forsake the non-gods they had worshiped.

Rahab was an example of someone in the second category. She welcomed Israelite spies into her home and hid them from the king's men (Josh. 2:1-7). When the king's men had gone on their way, Rahab said to Israel's spies, "I know that the Lord has given you the land, and that the fear of you has fallen upon us, and that all the inhabitants of the land melt away before you. For we have heard how the Lord dried up the water of the Red

A Red Cord in the Window

Sea before you when you came out of Egypt, and what you did to the two kings of the Amorites who were beyond the Jordan, to Sihon and Og, whom you devoted to destruction. And as soon as we heard it, our hearts melted, and there was no spirit left in any man because of you, for the Lord your God, he is God in the heavens above and on the earth beneath" (2:9-11).

The words of Rahab are words of faith (Heb. 11:31). She believed that the Lord was going to give the Promised Land to the Israelites; in fact, in her wording, the giving of the land was as good as done (Josh. 2:9). She believed that God had parted the Red Sea (2:10). In fact, she confessed Israel's God as the God of heaven and earth (2:11). By confessing Yahweh as Lord over the realms of heaven and earth, she was declaring her allegiance to Yahweh and rejecting the Canaanite idols.

While the spies were still in her home, Rahab made an urgent request: "Now then, please swear to me by the Lord that, as I have dealt kindly with you, you also will deal kindly with my father's house, and give me a sure sign that you will save alive my father and mother, my brothers and sisters, and all who belong to them, and deliver our lives from death" (Josh. 2:12-13). She believed that judgment was coming for the Canaanites, and that Yahweh was bringing it through the Israelite conquest of the land. For those who defied Yahweh's rule, they would reap death.

But Rahab, speaking also for her household, was not resistant to Yahweh's rule and the coming conquest. She simply wanted to make clear where she stood, so she pled for understanding and mercy. The men agreed to grant her request. They told her, "Behold, when we come into the land, you shall tie this scarlet cord in the window through which you let us down, and you shall gather into your house your father and mother, your brothers, and all your father's household. Then if anyone goes out of the doors of your house into the street, his blood shall be

A Red Cord in the Window

on his own head, and we shall be guiltless. But if a hand is laid on anyone who is with you in the house, his blood shall be on our head" (Josh. 2:18-19). So Rahab sent the men away, back to the Israelites, and she tied the scarlet cord in her window (2:21).

When the conquest began, and when Jericho would be the first city to fall, Joshua told the spies, "Go into the prostitute's house and bring out from there the woman and all who belong to her, as you swore to her" (Josh. 6:22). The scarlet cord would identify her home, and the judgment would pass over that house. Pass *over*. *Passover*. Have you noticed that there are thematic links between the Rahab story and the tenth plague?

God promised to bring judgment, to Egypt and to the Canaanites (starting with Jericho). And if someone appropriately marked their home, that act of faith would mean they—and everyone inside the home—would be spared from the coming judgment. In Exodus 12, the Israelites had to slay an unblemished lamb and put its blood on each home's doorposts and lintel. And in Joshua 2, Rahab had to put a scarlet cord in her window. Both the blood of the lamb and the scarlet cord were means of assurance for those in the home. Judgment would not fall on the homes that were marked by the appointed means—whether the unblemished lamb or the scarlet cord.

The events in Joshua 2 and 6, therefore, recalled the exodus from Egypt and God's deliverance through his appointed provision. Since the scarlet cord episode evoked the exodus, and since the exodus pointed forward to God's provision of his Son on the cross, the scarlet cord foreshadowed the substitutionary work of Christ. The cord is about the cross because through that provision the Lord delivers those who respond in faith.

The scarlet cord meant that the specific home was a refuge from judgment. And that's what the cross means about the Lord Jesus. He is a refuge for all who come to him and trust him.

95

A Red Cord in the Window

The good news of the gospel is not that God has provided a temporary refuge for sinners. He has given his only Son as an everlasting refuge. He saves us to the uttermost. No judgment shall fall on us, because on the cross, judgment fell on him.

Jesus was born into a world that was already under judgment. He came to call sinners to himself, and from his hands come the mercy of redemption and pardon. He said, "For God did not send his Son into the world to condemn the world, but in order that the world might be saved through him" (John 3:17).

22

Samson, the Mighty Judge

Before the Israelites had a king, they had judges. In the book of Judges, these figures were deliverers, saviors. After a cycle of Israel's rebellion, the Lord's punishment, and the people's repentance, the Lord would raise up a judge to rescue the people from their adversaries. The last judge in the book of Judges was named Samson. And Samson was a type of Christ.

The story of Samson spans Judges 13–16. The biblical author devotes an entire chapter to Samson's birth—first to its prediction, then to its fulfillment. Samson's mother was married to Manoah, and she was also barren (Judg. 13:2). The report of her barrenness sets up a miraculous conception, because the Bible reader has already seen what happens in the lives of Sarah and Rebekah and Rachel when the author reported their barrenness: the Lord overcame it (see Gen. 21; 25; 30).

Manoah's wife wasn't the final barren women identified in Scripture, but what happens with her indicates the important

Samson, the Mighty Judge

role her child would play. Samson would be a mighty judge. An angel prophesies his birth in Judges 13. The angel told Manoah's wife, "Behold, you are barren and have not borne children, but you shall conceive and bear a son" (Judg. 13:3). The announcement reminds us of the amazing news which Abraham and Sarah had received, when a heavenly figure foretold the birth of Isaac.

The woman's husband wasn't around to witness the angelic revelation, so he prayed that God would send the messenger again (Judg. 13:8-10). The angel confirmed the revelation to Manoah (13:11-14). And when the time had come, the woman gave birth to a son and named him Samson (13:24).

According to the biblical record, Samson had incredible strength, superior to all his enemies. But Samson's years as a judge were also fraught with character flaws and unjustifiable actions. For example, he rejected the wisdom of his parents about finding a mate and, instead, chose a wife from the daughters of the Philistines (Judg. 14:1-3). He ate honey from the body of a dead lion, a carcass which would have made Samson ceremonially unclean (14:8-9). Following a series of days that revolved around a riddle, Samson's wife ended up with his best man (14:20). Eventually, Samson lay with a prostitute in Gaza (16:1).

Perhaps the most interesting relationship of Samson's was with Delilah, whom the Philistines hoped could share with them his weakness so that they could triumph over him (Judg. 16:4-6). In a series of episodes between Samson and Delilah, he teased her with information and merely misled her (16:7-14). But after mounting emotional pressure, Samson confided the secret to his great strength: "A razor has never come upon my head, for I have been a Nazirite to God from my mother's womb. If my head is shaved, then my strength will leave me, and I shall

Samson, the Mighty Judge

become weak and be like any other man" (16:17). Samson's long hair symbolized the fact that he had been set apart, even before his birth, to live as a Nazirite.

Helping Samson go to sleep, she summoned a man who shaved the hair from Samson's head (Judg. 16:18-19). This time, he could not escape the clutches of the Philistines. They subdued him, gouging out his eyes and binding him with shackles (16:20-21). But as the days passed, his hair began to grow again. And the growth of the hair signaled the return of his strength.

One day, when the Philistine lords gathered for a pagan sacrifice, they summoned Samson for entertainment (Judg. 16:23-25). As he entertained them, he stood between pillars (16:25-26). Samson prayed, "O Lord God, please remember me and please strengthen me only this once, O God, that I may be avenged on the Philistines for my two eyes" (16:28). And he leaned with all his might against the pillars and said, "Let me die with the Philistines" (16:30). The house collapsed, killing everyone inside. The biblical author said, "So the dead whom he killed at his death were more than those whom he had killed during his life" (16:30).

Samson was a deeply flawed man, whose death ended the lives of his enemies. Even better would be a death that could reconcile enemies through salvation. Jesus is a true and greater Samson. Our Lord's birth was prophesied, but Mary was not a barren woman. When the angel appeared to Mary, she was unmarried and a virgin. The conception was miraculous. And the child who grew up was without sin. He didn't have a flawed character or commit lawless acts. The Lord Jesus kept the law perfectly.

During his earthly ministry, Jesus didn't topple Philistine armies. He gave sight to the blind and hearing to the deaf. He even raised the dead. Jesus' works were not of vengeance. They

Samson, the Mighty Judge

were works of restoration and transformation. Jesus stretched out his hands, not against two pillars but against the rugged grain of a wooden cross. There, raised up on a cross outside the city of Jerusalem, Jesus died. And when he died, others lived (Matt. 27:51-52). The substitutionary death of Jesus meant salvation, pardon for sinners. In Judges 16, Samson gave his life so that others would die for their sins. In the four Gospels, Jesus gave his life so that *he* could die for *our* sins.

The story of Samson is an incredible account of strength and fortitude. But Christ Jesus was greater. Peter told the people in Jerusalem, "Jesus of Nazareth, a man attested to you by God with mighty works and wonders and signs that God did through him in your midst, as you yourselves know—this Jesus, delivered up according to the definite plan and foreknowledge of God, you crucified and killed by the hands of lawless men. God raised him up, loosing the pangs of death, because it was not possible for him to be held by it" (Acts 2:22-24).

We needed a deliverer who could rescue us from something much worse than the Philistines. Christ Jesus was born to rescue us from sin and death and hell. He was born and lived and died. But what those around the cross that Friday afternoon couldn't perceive was the wonder Jesus was accomplishing and which he finished: atonement.

Jesus wasn't born to take life but to give life—*his* life.

23

Boaz, the Bethlehem Redeemer

Though the book of Judges was a partial record of spiritual waywardness in the land of Israel, God was at work, even in the darkness. According to the opening line of the book of Ruth, the subsequent story was in "the days when the judges ruled" (Ruth 1:1). Famine had gripped the Promised Land, so some people left to find food and livelihood elsewhere.

From Bethlehem, there was a family who traveled to Moab, where the mother's sons found wives (Ruth 1:2). But the woman's husband and sons died, so she, along with her daughters-in-law, became widows (1:3-5). When the older widow, who was called Naomi, was ready to return to Israel and to her home in Bethlehem, one of her daughters-in-law insisted on going with her (1:6-18). The insistent woman was Ruth, and she told

Boaz, the Bethlehem Redeemer

Naomi, "For where you go I will go, and where you lodge I will lodge. Your people shall be my people, and your God my God. Where you die I will die, and there will I be buried. May the Lord do so to me and more also if anything but death parts me from you" (1:16-17).

When Naomi and Ruth arrived in Bethlehem, Ruth desired to glean in a grainfield owned by someone who would look favorably upon her need (Ruth 2:1-2). Unintentionally, but certainly providentially, Ruth went to Boaz's field, and he showed her favor. In fact, he exceeded the requirements of the Law of Moses (2:6-10). He was very generous toward her, for he had heard of all that happened in Moab to her and to Naomi (2:11). He invited Ruth to share a meal with the reapers, eating bread and drinking wine (2:14). He permitted her to keep gleaning, and he ordered that no one should intervene as she did so (2:15).

Ruth returned home that evening with a massive amount of barley (Ruth 2:17-18). When Naomi learned about the location and the owner of the field, she said, "The man is a close relative of ours, one of our redeemers" (2:20). A kinsman redeemer could come alongside oppressed or needy family members and remedy their situation. In the eyes of Naomi, Boaz not only had food that she and Ruth could receive, she believed Boaz and Ruth should marry. And she instructed Ruth accordingly, talking about a threshing floor where Boaz would be alone and could be approached (3:1-5).

When Ruth arrived at the threshing floor, she did not act inappropriately. She told Boaz, "I am Ruth, your servant. Spread your wings over your servant, for you are a redeemer" (Ruth 3:9). Boaz knew that a nearer relative would need to have the option of acting as a kinsman redeemer (3:12). But Boaz was ready to fulfill the role if the other relative was unwilling (3:13).

Boaz, the Bethlehem Redeemer

He treated Ruth with dignity and upheld her honor, directing her to leave before the sunrise so that nothing unseemly would be assumed by others (3:13-14).

In the climax of the narrative, Boaz indeed married Ruth, and together they had a child (Ruth 4:13). The journey of the book is from emptiness to a new kind of fullness. Boaz was the redeemer who welcomed Ruth under the shadow of his wings. He was like the Lord in that way, for the Lord drew the Israelites under his wings, under his protection and covenant faithfulness. Boaz's actions toward Ruth are especially distinct when we remember that she was a Moabite. She was a Gentile who left her pagan idols and household and then journeyed to the Promised Land for a new life. Her redemption by Boaz secured her future and livelihood.

The redemption theme connects Boaz with Yahweh, for Yahweh was Israel's great redeemer. Formerly captives in Egypt, the Israelites enjoyed the freedom of redemption under the shadow of Yahweh's wings. Not only does Boaz remind us, in a micro sense, of the larger role which God played in Israel's redemption, he is a man who points forward to a greater redeemer.

According to John the Baptist's father Zechariah, the birth of John meant the dawning of redemption, for God had made promises in the Old Testament that he was keeping. Zechariah said, "Blessed be the Lord God of Israel, for he has visited and redeemed his people and has raised up a horn of salvation for us in the house of his servant David" (Luke 1:68-69). The good news about John's birth is that it prepared the way for the Messiah.

After Jesus was born, Mary and Joseph presented him at the Jerusalem temple, where a man named Simeon said, "For my eyes have seen your salvation that you have prepared in the

Boaz, the Bethlehem Redeemer

presence of all peoples, a light for revelation to the Gentiles and for glory to your people Israel" (Luke 2:30-32). Into our spiritual poverty and deep darkness, God shined everlasting light. While Boaz gave light and hope to Ruth, Jesus gives light and hope to the nations.

Jesus is the redeemer we needed. He not only kept God's law, his mercy and compassion exceeded the requirements of the law in the way he treated others. He took a bride from the nations—the Church, a people whom he purchased from every tribe and tongue. When God sent his Son to us, Jesus was born in the same place where Boaz had lived. This was the same town which the scribes identified when they answered Herod the Great's question. He had asked where the Christ was to be born (Matt. 2:4), and they quoted Micah 5:2 to him (Matt. 2:5-6). The Christ would be born in Bethlehem.

When we read about a blessed and merciful redeemer from Bethlehem, who kept God's law and who took a bride from the nations, we are reading a story about Boaz. But in the fullness of God's Word, the story of Boaz becomes the story of the Christ. The Lord Jesus was born to gather us under the refuge of his redeeming wings. For our spiritual emptiness, he is our fullness. To our desperate condition, he comes with steadfast mercy and strength.

24

David, the Singing King

The book of Ruth ends with a genealogy, and the last name in the list is David. He would be the first king of Judah's tribe, because his predecessor (Saul) was from the tribe of Benjamin. But David's childhood in Bethlehem didn't exactly indicate that he would rule a nation. In 1 Samuel 16, we learn that David was the youngest of eight sons (1 Sam. 16:10). Through the prophet Samuel, the Lord passed over all of the siblings until, at last, David was anointed (16:12-13). Coinciding with this anointing, the Spirit of the Lord came upon David to equip and empower him (16:13).

But David's rise to power was not quick, nor was it easy. As a young man from Bethlehem, he entered into King Saul's service (1 Sam. 16:14-23). David was musically talented (16:23), and he was physically competent enough to have overcome both lions and bears during his earlier years as a shepherd (17:34-36). Facing a Philistine giant from Gath named Goliath, David

David, the Singing King

stood his ground and, to the surprise of everyone, subdued the mighty warrior (17:48-51). David seemed fearless and devoted to Yahweh's glory.

During the remainder of Saul's reign, David had to evade the king's snares, for Saul wanted to kill him. The Lord spared David's life, and multiple times David spared Saul's life. When David was approximately thirty years old, he became king over the whole land of Israel (2 Sam. 5:3-5). God made a covenant with David to raise up a descendant, a son, who would occupy the throne forever (7:12-13). From that point on, David lived and reigned and even wrote songs in light of the covenant promise that God had made.

David was a singer and composer. Approximately half of the psalms in the book of Psalms were written by him. We learn from the biblical narratives and the psalms that David was a suffering king. There was tragedy within his family, rebellion from children, and conspiracy against him. He even had to flee Jerusalem, exiled from the city where he reigned. Yet God vindicated David and triumphed over his enemies. According to 2 Samuel 23:1, David was "the man who was raised on high, the anointed of the God of Jacob, the sweet psalmist of Israel."

As the sweet psalmist of Israel, David's compositions provided the words and patterns that would be fulfilled by his greater Son. In Psalm 16, David wrote about not being abandoned to corruption (Ps. 16:10). In Psalm 22, he wrote words of groaning and cried out for the nearness of God's favor (Ps. 22:1-2, 24). In Psalm 110, he spoke about the future Anointed One hearing the words: "Sit at my right hand, until I make your enemies your footstool" (Ps. 110:1).

In the Lord's providence, the life of David became a large royal pattern of suffering and vindication which Jesus would fulfill. According to the opening line of Matthew's Gospel,

David, the Singing King

Jesus is the "son of David" (Matt. 1:1), so the Davidic emphasis is evident right away. Jesus was from the tribe of Judah and from David's lineage (1:2-17). Furthermore, Jesus was born in David's town—the town of Bethlehem. Though Jesus' mother, Mary, was from Nazareth, the Lord's sovereignty ensured, through a decree from Caesar about a census, that the birth would take place at the right time and at the right location (Luke 2:1-5).

So the King of kings was born in a seemingly insignificant village. But the story of David in 1–2 Samuel shows us that, in God's hands, the last can become first, for the last-born son of Jesse became the king of all Israel. Born in Bethlehem and growing up in Nazareth, Jesus' childhood didn't seem marked by royal fanfare. Yet he was the promised Son of 2 Samuel 7:12-14, the one who would rule on his father David's throne forever.

Jesus was a rejected king, however. He came to his own, yet his own did not receive him (John 1:11). Some of his contemporaries proclaimed him to be the Son of David (Matt. 20:30; 21:9), but they didn't fully understand what the mission of his kingship would involve. He was the Son of David, but he was also the Son of Man who would suffer and die at the hands of the Jewish leaders and Roman authorities (Mark 10:33-34).

Even Jesus' disciples didn't grasp the entirety of what his mission entailed. They did confess him to be the Christ—the king—but then Peter recoiled at Jesus' teaching that the Christ would suffer and die (Matt. 16:13-23). Like David, Jesus was the exiled king. But the rejection of Jesus was part of the divine plan to secure the enthronement of Jesus. He would be exalted through humiliation. His suffering would lead to glory.

On the cross, Jesus quoted some Psalms of David, for those words most fully and appropriately belonged on his lips (Matt. 27:46; John 19:28). Even the Golgotha scene of being

David, the Singing King

surrounded by enemies and gambling soldiers recalled the life and suffering of David (Ps. 22:16-18; Mark 15:22-24). Through suffering, he triumphed. In death, he overcame. The vindication of the cross was Jesus' resurrection of the dead. Indeed, it was through his bodily resurrection that he could reign forever on the throne as the Son of David. Throughout ancient history and in our modern day, a king's rule inevitably ends because the king will die. But rising from death, Jesus overcame the cords of corruption. With glorified bodily life, he could reign without end.

When the angel Gabriel came to Mary with news of a future son, part of the heavenly revelation was about the Davidic hope. Gabriel said, "And the Lord God will give to him the throne of his father David, and he will reign over the house of Jacob forever, and of his kingdom there will be no end" (Luke 1:32-33).

Though the angel's news was wonderful, Mary would not have fully processed what would transpire in order for the child to grow up and occupy an everlasting throne. But she treasured the promise in her heart. And when the time came for Joseph to go to Bethlehem, she went with him. She made it to the town still pregnant, ready to give birth at any time. She was on the eve of something wonderful.

25

Solomon, the Wise Son of David

Long before Jesus was the Son of David, Solomon was the son of David. After his father, Solomon was king over Israel for forty years. His reign began well. He was a wise king as the result of an answered prayer. God had told him, "Ask what I shall give you" (1 Kings 3:5). And Solomon said, "Give your servant therefore an understanding mind to govern your people, that I may discern between good and evil, for who is able to govern this your great people?" (3:9).

The Lord agreed to Solomon's request: "Behold, I now do according to your word. Behold, I give you a wise and discerning mind, so that none like you has been before you and none like you shall arise after you" (1 Kings 3:12). God's promise, then, was that Solomon's wisdom would be supreme. He was like a new Adam, possessing a discerning mind and exercising dominion. The Lord greatly blessed him with a prosperous and peaceful reign. In applying his wisdom, Solomon composed

Solomon, the Wise Son of David

proverbs and songs (4:32) to nourish the faith and future of God's people.

King Solomon's wisdom became part of his international reputation: "And people of all nations came to hear the wisdom of Solomon, and from all the kings of the earth, who had heard of his wisdom" (1 Kings 4:34). When the queen of Sheba learned about Solomon's wisdom, she traveled to hear him in person, bringing with her hard questions to test him (10:1). Her interaction with Solomon exceeded her expectations (10:6-7). She also gifted him with much gold, a great quantity of spices, and many precious stones (10:10). These were offerings fit for a great king, especially a wise and renowned king like Solomon.

Besides answering hard questions and composing proverbs and songs, the wisdom of Solomon was displayed in his oversight of a massive construction project. He oversaw the building of the Jerusalem temple, which replaced the tabernacle. His father David had earlier brought the ark of the covenant to Jerusalem (2 Sam. 6), and now the temple would function as the sanctuary. The king was a temple builder (1 Kings 6-8).

While Solomon was the son of David, he wasn't the promised Son of David from 2 Samuel 7:12-13. We know, from 1 Kings 11, for example, that Solomon did foolish things. He took many concubines to himself and amassed many chariots (1 Kings 10:26–11:3), deeds which violate the divine stipulations for Israel's king (see Deut. 17:14-20). According to 1 Kings 11, "For when Solomon was old his wives turned away his heart after other gods, and his heart was not wholly true to the Lord his God, as was the heart of David his father" (1 Kings 11:4).

The Lord told Solomon, "Since this has been your practice and you have not kept my covenant and my statutes that I have commanded you, I will surely tear the kingdom from you and

Solomon, the Wise Son of David

will give it to your servant" (1 Kings 11:11). Solomon would not be the king who would rule forever. Therefore, the covenant promise of a forever Davidic king would transcend Solomon's reign and be fulfilled in someone else.

The true and greater Solomon was Jesus. He was the Son of David (Matt. 1:1) and lived with his heart truly and wholly devoted to God's commandments. The four Gospels highlight the wisdom of Jesus, which surpassed the clever traps of his adversaries and which instructed his followers about the kingdom of heaven. He once told some scribes and Pharisees, "The queen of the South will rise up at the judgment with this generation and condemn it, for she came from the ends of the earth to hear the wisdom of Solomon, and behold, something greater than Solomon is here" (Matt. 12:42).

Jesus' words in Matthew 12:42 drew attention to Solomon's wisdom and how a queen had traveled to hear it. When Jesus compared himself to Solomon, he said, "Something greater than Solomon is here," so his claim is to be a person of even greater wisdom. In Luke 2:40, the biblical author talked about Jesus' childhood when he said "the child grew and became strong, filled with wisdom. And the favor of God was upon him." Later in Luke 2 we read, "And Jesus increased in wisdom and in stature and in favor with God and man" (Luke 2:52).

The promised king and greater Solomon had arrived. And Jesus, like Solomon, was a temple builder. But his temple wasn't what the Israelites were used to seeing. He referred to his own body as a temple which would be torn down and then rebuilt (John 2:19), language foreshadowing his crucifixion and resurrection (2:21-22). But he also referred to his disciples as a group he was building. He said, "I will build my church, and the gates of hell shall not prevail against it" (Matt. 16:18). Jesus was building a temple—the church. Every believer is a living

Solomon, the Wise Son of David

stone which Jesus joins to other living stones (believers) as he builds a spiritual house (1 Pet. 2:5). Solomon's temple fell to Babylon. Jesus' temple will not fall—not even to the fury of hell itself. Jesus is the faithful and wise temple builder, a new and better Solomon.

Echoes of Solomon's story begin quite early in Jesus' life. Think about the magi who traveled far to see him. Like the queen of Sheba in 1 Kings 10, the magi were searching for the great king. And they, too, brought gifts to give to the Christ child: "And going into the house, they saw the child with Mary his mother, and they fell down and worshiped him. Then, opening their treasures, they offered him gifts, gold and frankincense and myrrh" (Matt. 2:11). These were not normal gifts for a child, but they were certainly gifts fit for a great king.

Before the child could talk, before his hands did signs and wonders, and before he summoned sinners to follow him, he was worshiped in Bethlehem by Gentiles from a far land. Something great had happened to the world. Light had dawned in the darkness, and the darkness would not overcome it. The child of Bethlehem is Lord of heaven and earth. All glory and wisdom, all honor and power, all blessing and praise, belong to him, forever and ever.